LEADERSHIP
DNA

LEADERSHIP
DNA

BOOK TWO

Recognizing Good and Poor Leadership
in the Real World

PAUL OKUM

LEADERSHIP DNA, BOOK TWO
RECOGNIZING GOOD AND POOR
LEADERSHIP IN THE REAL WORLD

iUniverse books may be ordered through booksellers or by contacting:

iUniverse
1663 Liberty Drive
Bloomington, IN 47403
www.iuniverse.com
1-800-Authors (1-800-288-4677)

Because of the dynamic nature of the Internet, any web addresses or links contained in this book may have changed since publication and may no longer be valid. The views expressed in this work are solely those of the author and do not necessarily reflect the views of the publisher, and the publisher hereby disclaims any responsibility for them.

Any people depicted in stock imagery provided by Thinkstock are models, and such images are being used for illustrative purposes only.
Certain stock imagery © Thinkstock.

ISBN: 978-1-4917-6453-4 (sc)
ISBN: 978-1-4917-6407-7 (hc)
ISBN: 978-1-4917-6454-1 (e)

Library of Congress Control Number: 2015919676

Print information available on the last page.

iUniverse rev. date: 03/30/2016

CONTENTS

Introduction 1

PART 1: BUSINESS AND
PERSONNEL MANAGEMENT

1: Doing What We Were Meant to Do 9

2: Good Leadership Drives an Imperfect Decision. 13

3: Effective Negotiations Are Characterized by
   Compromise and Moving Forward 15

4: Seven Words That Can Ruin Any Organization 19

5: Good Leaders Are Not Constrained by the Facts 21

6: Organization Charts Institute Hierarchy and
   Control at a Price 23

7: Good Leadership Cannot Be Choreographed. 27

8: Good Leaders and Parents Have Similar Goals for
   Their Children, Employees, and Citizens 29

9: Good Leaders Understand the Interdependence of
   Government and Business 31

10: The Solitary Nature of Leadership 35

11: Dealing with the Intolerable Boss 39

12: Good Leadership Does Not Come Attached to a
    Diploma 43

13: Leaders Can Benefit from the US Marines' "Rule of
    Three" 47

14: Trying Your Best Is Not Good Enough 51

15: It's Easier to Ask for Forgiveness Than to Ask for
Permission. 53

16: Competition and Cooperation: Good Leaders
Recognize the Need for Both 57

17: Being a Good Leader Is Much More Than an Eight-
to-Five Job. 61

18: Team Synergy Challenged by Work-from-Home
Programs. 63

19: Good Leaders Have the "Right Stuff" 67

20: Succession Planning: A Critical Aspect of Good
Leadership. 69

21: Good Leaders Rise above Adversity and Bad Breaks 73

22: George Washington: A Profile of Innate Leadership
Talent 75

23: Good leadership Is the Prerequisite for Success 77

24: Good Leaders Will Confront Difficult Issues 79

25: Good Leaders Utilize the What-If Exercise in Planning. . .81

26: The Double-Edged Sword of Employee Recognition . . .83

27: Employees Who Assess Their Leadership Skills
Will Compare Themselves with the Worst Leaders,
Not the Best 87

28: The Importance of Employee Orientations,
Especially for New Employees. .91

29: A Key Piece of Good Leadership Is Reengineering
      Work Processes. 95

30: The Negative Impact of a Micromanager on an
      Organization and Its Employees 99

31: Dealing with the Problem Employee. 103

PART 2: GOVERNMENT AND POLITICS

32: Mediocre Leadership Has Become the New Normal. . . 109

33: Compromise: A Bridge to Agreement or a Sign of
      Weakness 111

34: You Can't Lead Looking in the Rearview Mirror 115

35: Rugged Individualism versus Community Outreach:
      Competing Philosophies in America. 117

36: Good Leadership Ensures That America's Best Days
      Are Always Today and Tomorrow. 121

37: The Poor, the Middle Class, and the Rich in
      Classless America 123

38: Good Leaders Will Not Allow America to Be Held
      Hostage to Political Agendas. 125

39: The Self-Righteous Minority 127

40: A Warning from George Washington about Political
      Parties 131

Conclusion 135

Appendix 137

Bibliography 145

Index 147

INTRODUCTION

In my book *Leadership DNA: Why the Accepted Premise That Anyone Can Be a Leader Is Utterly False and the Main Cause of Poor Leadership in America*, I stated that the predominant view of leadership in America has been for generations, and continues to be, that leadership is a commonplace skill that anyone can learn. According to the leadership gurus and a host of leadership books, anyone can be a leader if he or she has the desire to be a leader, a commitment to work hard, and leadership training. Each leadership guru has a personal formula for creating a leader. These formulas are laid out in great detail in book after book, with volumes of pseudoscientific evidence presented to support each guru's step-by-step plans to mass-produce good leaders. There's just one problem: their formulas don't work.

Despite the claims of these often high-profile gurus, their formulas, and the billions of dollars spent each year to train and produce assembly-line leaders, America is suffering from a leadership vacuum. The much-promised results from applying these formulas have not materialized into an abundance of good leaders. Quite the contrary—the persistent low approval ratings of our political leaders and the negative results of employee surveys all point to a high level of dissatisfaction with our leaders in both the public and private sectors of American society.

Leadership DNA rejects the premise that leaders are made and instead argues that we are all born as unique individuals with a set of unique talents that are transferred through DNA from our biological parents. Consequently, because of this uniqueness, not everyone will possess innate leadership talent, and without that particular talent, it doesn't matter how many leadership books a person reads, how many workshops a person attends, or how much leadership experience a person has. Most people will never become good leaders, because they lack innate leadership talent. *You can put a person in a leadership position, but you can't put leadership in the person.*

We've all either experienced working for a poor leader or witnessed the devastating effect a poor leader can have on an organization and the people in it. During my forty-year career in leadership positions and as a human resources director, I saw too many technically skilled and highly valued employees placed into leadership positions only to be turned into intolerable bosses who did not have a clue how to lead. The gurus, their formulas, and the professional leadership trainers have failed in their efforts to turn everyone into leaders. The primary reason for this failure is that these formulas are based on an effort to use science to define leadership, placing good leaders' behaviors and traits under a microscope in an attempt to extract and replicate the ingredients that make up good leaders. The leadership gurus have completely dismissed or ignored the fact that leadership is not a science. Instead, it's an art form and, as such, defies scientific analysis.

To improve the leadership in America, we need to stop trying to make everyone into a leader and instead focus on ways to identify and develop natural-born leaders with innate leadership talent. In this effort, the focus must change from a concentration on science as the answer to America's leadership vacuum, to a discussion regarding leadership as an art. Artists tap into their personal reservoir of innate talent and generate a level of creativity and spontaneity that scientific formulas cannot define or measure. *The science of leadership argues incorrectly that leaders can be made by simply following step-by-step formulas and that leadership is a commonplace skill that can be learned by anyone. However, the art of leadership argues that leaders are born as unique individuals with a set of unique talents. The leadership gurus' equation (personal desire + commitment + leadership training = real leadership) is fundamentally flawed because it does not account for innate leadership talent and the uniqueness of each person. Once individual talent is factored in, then the valid equation will read: desire + commitment + leadership training + innate leadership talent = real leadership.*

Leadership DNA is both a philosophical discussion on the science and art of leadership and also a practical guidebook that describes numerous signposts to assist in the effort to identify and develop natural-born leaders who have the God-given leadership DNA to be good leaders. However, in the final analysis, the only way to know if a person is a born leader is by placing the person into a leadership position and observing the individual's performance, including dealing with the stress and challenges of leadership. Leadership training can enhance the talent with which a person was born, but it cannot put the talent in a person if it doesn't already exist.

Regarding identifying natural-born leaders, Thomas Jefferson said, "The Creator has not thought proper to mark those on the forehead who are of the stuff to make good generals." Clearly Jefferson recognized and accepted the existence of innate leadership talent, or "stuff," and he understood that leadership was not inherent in everyone. Jefferson recognized that the only way to know if a person had leadership talent was to put the person in command and observe how he or she reacted to the leadership challenges of war.

The *Leadership DNA* guidebook encompasses how to

- examine a person's motives and behavior patterns for the potential of leadership talent,
- identify and select natural-born leaders,
- deal with the aloneness of being a leader,
- incorporate leadership talent scouts into the leadership team,
- handle the challenges of first-time leaders,
- consider feedback on a leader's performance,
- give clear directions and a set of guiding principles, and
- deal with poor leaders and other leadership-related topics.

In *Leadership DNA, Book Two,* I apply the art-of-leadership concepts discussed in the *Leadership DNA* guidebook to leadership situations and challenges, and I describe what good and poor leaders do when faced with these crises. As a nation, America needs good leaders in every part of society, with special emphasis on government and industry; they must possess innate leadership talent as one of their unique DNA talents, and they must accept the tremendous responsibility that comes with this particular talent.

America needs natural-born leaders more than ever in today's rapidly changing world; they must be capable of effectively dealing with a wide range of issues without tearing our country apart in the process. Too many people in leadership positions are driven by their own personal or ideological interests. Too many politicians and corporate CEOs are more focused on winning elections or making profits at any cost while rationalizing their behavior as the end justifies the means. Our nation's best interests are sacrificed for a victory at the ballot box or in the corporate boardroom.

Radical conservatives and liberals turn every issue into some sort of crusade where Americans are repeatedly asked to pick which side they support. In this environment, there is neither a moderate middle ground nor a willingness to compromise. All candidates preach that their views, their "truths," are the only right ones, and if you don't agree, then you are viewed as un-American. This polarization of America produces gridlock within Congress and between Congress and the White House. Good leaders understand that America needs leaders who will champion real debate on issues and ensure that the best interests of the nation come first.

Correspondingly, in workplaces across this country, from small businesses to large corporations, America needs leaders who will balance their desires for an unrestrained *free-market system* and high-profit margins for a few, with a *fair-market system* with appropriate checks and balances to ensure a level playing field for all. Employers need the freedom to operate so that their businesses can stay profitable, while recognizing that employees are not just a set of mindless hands to simply do a job. Good leaders will invest in their workers and continually prepare them for current and future challenges. To maintain a strong America, we must have a strong economy, and that is possible only if we have a vibrant business community within the United States. To attain this, there must be good leadership at all levels of government and industry. And intolerable bosses and unsatisfactory employees must be dealt with quickly, or they will destroy an organization from within.

The goals of *Leadership DNA, Book Two* are to expand on some topics in *Leadership DNA*, emphasize the art of leadership over the science of leadership, and provide real-world examples of how good leaders act to ensure that the leadership needs of our republic are met by natural-born leaders who will not shrink from their responsibilities to safeguard and promote the United States of America first and foremost.

Given these goals, *Book Two* is intended for anyone currently in a leadership position and for those contemplating moving into leadership positions. It contains forty short essays dealing with a wide range of real-world topics and issues. These essays are designed to stand alone and can be read in any order. I've grouped the essays into two main categories: "Business and Personnel Management" and "Government and Politics." However, the essays are difficult to compartmentalize, and the material will often overlap because leadership permeates such a wide range of human endeavor and is the common denominator for these essays. Once the reader has read these topical essays, what should be clear is that regardless of the situation or issue, as long as there are natural-born leaders in leadership positions, America and Americans benefit as individuals, citizens, employees, and a nation. When poor leaders occupy leadership positions, American innovation and initiative suffer, because poor leaders lack the talent to be successful in leadership positions.

PART 1

BUSINESS AND PERSONNEL MANAGEMENT

1

DOING WHAT WE WERE MEANT TO DO

Any discussion about leadership and how natural-born leaders respond to leadership challenges must start with an understanding that to be really good at something we must possess the corresponding level of innate talent. Within our unique set of inherited talents, we have the ability to excel at these activities, but because each person is unique, everyone cannot excel at everything. We don't like to face this truth, because we were raised believing that if we want something badly enough, are willing to work hard to get it, and receive training or coaching in the subject, then we can be anything we want to be. This is a false dream. Colin Powell, former chairman of the Joint Chiefs of Staff and secretary of state, said, "That's what you really have to look for in life, something that you like and something that you think you're pretty good at. And if you can put these two things together, then you're on the right track and just drive on." Johann Wolfgang von Goethe, a German statesman and writer, also said regarding this topic, "The person born with a talent they are meant to use will find their greatest happiness in using it." In other words, do what you are passionate about and good at, and that will allow your natural talents to express themselves.

Consider the women and men who represent their countries in the Olympics. For everyone who competes, there are thousands of competitors who do not have the level of talent required to make the final cut and win the right to compete in the Olympics. Those women and men who are unsuccessful in the preliminary competitions have the desire, commitment, and training, but at some level of competition they fell short, while others who possess more talent made it to the Olympics. Further, out of all those who represent their countries, only an elite few actually win medals.

The Olympics is just one example among many where some individuals have their dreams and aspirations realized, but the cold, hard reality is that most do not; they simply run out of talent at some lower level of competition. An argument can be made that injuries play a role or one coach may be a little better than another, but that does not change the overall conclusion that talent and the degree to which a person possesses it are the determining factors in how accomplished that person will be in a particular activity.

Likewise with leadership, heredity bestows upon us none, some, or a high degree of leadership talent. We need to do a good self-examination of our own talents and stop kidding ourselves that we can do or be anything we want. Instead, we must look inward and aim to discover what talents we actually possess. Good leaders know that the more we can align our careers, lives, or some aspect of them with the talents with which we were born, the more content and successful we will become, because we will be doing something we were meant to do—what we were born to do. We won't turn into intolerable bosses who clearly lack the innate leadership talent to be good leaders. But if we insist that gurus and formulas can make us all into leaders, then we will continue to mass-produce nonleaders who will not answer this nation's call for real leadership.

2

GOOD LEADERSHIP DRIVES
AN IMPERFECT DECISION

Good leaders in all segments of American society recognize that they have a responsibility to establish an environment and culture that become the generators of invention, innovation, and informed decision making. *Good leaders don't just make decisions; they make decisions better.* Good leaders are the catalysts who bring divergent points of view to the table for discussion, who ensure that all interests are represented, and who define the issues and set the parameters for the decisions to be formulated. From this crucible, there will emerge the ingredients for an informed, collaborative decision. How these ingredients are blended together by the leader is an art and will ultimately determine if a consensus can be reached.

Good leaders understand that each person or group supports their own "perfect" proposals on the issues and will argue for adoption with only minor modifications. They believe that their proposals represent the perfect solution, the right decision. Good leaders realize that any absolutist stance is the precursor of gridlock and paralysis. It takes skillful leaders to restate the objective and convince everyone that there are no perfect plans or decisions. The real question is how much "imperfection" is each person or group willing to accept. How much compromise is everyone willing to engage in to put the good of the many above the good of the few?

The role of the leader is to work with all involved to find the point that balances cold reality with the impassioned idealism of any proclaimed perfect decision. Of paramount importance is that leaders must thoroughly review the competing "perfect" proposals and make the difficult, clear-cut decisions required to move the organization and the country forward. Failure to do this will perpetuate internal squabbling and encourage opponents to find ways to scuttle the entire process, consciously or subconsciously.

When dialogue and debate fail to bring consensus, the leader must take command and reinvigorate the process with a sense of urgency to drive to the best possible imperfect decision for the greater good. This applies to government, business, finance, and so forth. Democracy is by its very nature chaotic and imperfect, as it struggles to respect and consider all opinions and options. Doing nothing is not an option in a world that is constantly changing and generating new and increasingly complex issues that good leaders must deal with if America is to remain strong.

3

EFFECTIVE NEGOTIATIONS ARE CHARACTERIZED BY COMPROMISE AND MOVING FORWARD

As a director of human resources, I participated in a variety of negotiations. These experiences taught me that there are certain procedures or protocols that, if followed, will increase the likelihood of reaching an agreement. In general, constructive and disciplined negotiations can assist in keeping everyone focused on finding ways to work together to create win-win solutions.

- To be successful, negotiators on both sides must clearly understand the impact on the organizations and the people they represent if the negotiators fail to reach an agreement. *When negotiating, winning cannot become more important than agreeing.*

- It is critical that both sides in a negotiation agree on a definition of the issues and the scope of the negotiations. Without agreement on these points, personal agendas typically take over the negotiations.
- Publicly professing rigid ideologies and proposals prior to and during negotiations leaves little room for any kind of meaningful dialogue and compromise on the issues. The negotiating table is no place to espouse a take-it-or-leave-it agenda.
- Everything cannot be a must-have win for one side at the negotiating table. All negotiators must embrace a willingness to compromise or else win-win solutions will not materialize.
- Both sides presenting a partisan assessment on how the negotiations are proceeding to the public or in a daily update is not conducive to building trust between the negotiating officials. It is counterproductive to publicly attack the person or persons with whom you are negotiating. Openly condemning each other builds resentment and makes it harder to reach an agreement.
- The final outcome should not be a victory for one group and a defeat for the other. For negotiations to be successful and lasting, both parties must have obtained something that was important to them and their respective constituents. A slam dunk by one side over the other will only breed animosity and a desire for retribution. At the next negotiating session it will be much more difficult to fashion an agreement.

America needs good leaders who are capable of recognizing that the way forward is through win-win compromise. If we cannot sincerely negotiate in good faith via compromise, then we jeopardize the well-being of our government and business community, and we will suffer the consequences of allowing the interests of the few to override the interests of the many, not only in negotiations but in everything we do.

4

SEVEN WORDS THAT CAN RUIN ANY ORGANIZATION

The seven words that will make any good leader cringe are "But we've always done it that way." These words are especially debilitating to an organization, because they sap the innovation and initiative out of a workforce. But what's most important and disturbing is that the people who say these words are actually mirroring the attitude of their leaders. *A workforce is a reflection of its leadership, or, put another way, leadership gets the workforce it deserves.*

Consequently, when a good leader takes over an organization and hears these dreadful seven words emanating from the workforce, he or she will recognize that the people are simply parroting the words, actions, and inactions of the previous leadership. Such organizations and workforces have been mired in a poor leadership–induced, static environment where innovation and initiative are often discouraged or at the very least ignored.

Maintaining the status quo, whether consciously or unconsciously, is the standard of poor leadership. "If it ain't broke, don't fix it" is typically the mantra of poor leaders.

To eradicate the words "But we've always done it that way" and the mind-set they represent, good leaders must first reorient the leadership of an organization to understand that they now live in a world that is changing at an exponential rate and that leaders and workforces must change and adapt to stay relevant and "open for business." Often the organization's top leaders rush out to hold employee meetings in an attempt to convince the workforce of the need to change before they first obtain the buy-in of their own subordinate leaders.

While the workforce may sense the need to change, it's leadership that must drive the change and get the organization moving again and focused on the need to do things differently. Good leaders must alter the environment and culture within which their workforces function to induce the desired change in behavior or conduct. However, any change in a workforce will be temporary and fleeting until the employees see that their leaders have completely adopted the new direction in attitude, word, and deed. Only then will the seven words and their destructive way of thinking be eradicated.

5

GOOD LEADERS ARE NOT CONSTRAINED BY THE FACTS

According to the dictionary, a fact is a statement of truth. However, the truth about a particular thing or circumstance can change and thus change the facts. John F. Kennedy once said, "Change is the law of life. And those who look only to the past or present are certain to miss the future." And his brother Robert F. Kennedy said, "There are those who look at things the way they are and ask why ... I dream of things that never were, and ask why not." Both of these men knew that most people see the world as it is, but good leaders see the world as it could be.

Opinions, perspectives, and beliefs constantly change, and good leaders must be able to see beyond the facts of the past and the present and create a new future based on new realities. The existence of the Berlin Wall and the Communist Soviet Union were once facts, but no more. Once man could only peer at the sky and speculate; now we've traveled to the moon and beyond, discovering new truths, new facts. Real leaders are not content with being bound by yesterday's and today's realities.

To stay vibrant and competitive, businesses, governments, and nations must be challenged to move forward with a purpose, to evolve, and to continually reengineer themselves. A team, an organization, and a country will have a tendency to remain at rest until a force, a good leader, comes along to jump-start them and, by sheer force of will, get them moving again. The laws of physics applies to human beings and nations. Once moving, good leaders will drive the changes needed to maintain the momentum, and in the process they will be creating new perspectives and facts; from a candle to electricity, from a telegraph to an iPhone, the change in reality is immense.

On the other hand, poor leaders will allow themselves to be held captive by the facts of the past and present and thereby lock themselves into a particular paradigm or perspective. *Poor leaders work within the current system of facts; good leaders change the system and create new facts, new realities. Poor leaders remain at rest; good leaders realize that if you rest you rust.*

6

ORGANIZATION CHARTS
INSTITUTE HIERARCHY
AND CONTROL AT A PRICE

The use of organization charts in government offices and businesses is widespread. These charts are intended to represent and display an organization's formal management hierarchy or chain of command and define the authorized flow of communications up and down this hierarchy. The larger the organization, the more levels will be identified on these organization charts. Many of these organization charts typically have four or more levels encompassing supervisors, managers, and executives, all with a corresponding set of organizational job titles. This pyramid-like superstructure is installed over the workforce.

While this concept of operation will definitely ensure management control of work and people, good leaders understand that there are a multitude of problems associated with operating under the weight of these hierarchal structures:

- Each layer of managers has a tendency to filter the communications going up the chain of command to put themselves in the best light and also place their own spin on communications coming down the chain.

- Management officials typically believe that passing problem cases or policy issues to their bosses for discussion or resolution will reflect poorly on them. Consequently, there is a natural inclination by managers to procrastinate on raising issues up the chain until they have been thoroughly vetted at the lower levels. This process often takes an inordinate amount of time and can negatively impact the mission of the organization.

- Adherence to the protocol of a formal hierarchy often stifles innovation and initiative from the workforce because of the multiple levels of coordination and approval required to obtain changes to policy or operating procedures. Delegations of authority are often minimal, and decision making is normally retained at the upper levels of the organization at the expense of the first-level leaders and the workforce, where the work is actually being performed.

- Over time there is a loss of a sense of urgency to deal with issues raised, and instead many managers are content with maintaining the status quo because of the difficulty of getting someone to make a decision. Even the smallest issue requires an extensive wait time for resolution.

- Risk taking is discouraged, because this implies experimenting outside of the command and control boundaries of the organization. However, what is overlooked is that the absence of risk taking locks in organizational mediocrity.

Consequently, a structure with a strong centralized decision-making apparatus comes at a high price. Good leaders will push for an organizational structure that eliminates much of middle management and thereby flattens the structures. The corresponding hierarchy will be more responsive to customer and employee needs and will balance the desire for control with initiative, risk taking, and innovation. Key decision makers need to be close to their first-line leaders and workforces to stay abreast of the fast-changing workplace and world within which organizations must operate. Good leaders recognize this need for change; poor leaders seek the status quo.

7

GOOD LEADERSHIP CANNOT
BE CHOREOGRAPHED

For decades, leadership gurus have effectively convinced the vast majority of people that anyone can become a leader provided they have a personal desire to be a leader, a commitment to work hard to become a leader, and complete leadership training. These gurus have monopolized the field of leadership training, and they have each developed their own personal blueprints or formulas with the pledge that, if followed, the trainees will become good leaders. These step-by-step plans and formulas for success have been advocated in a multitude of leadership books, workshops, and seminars. These plans and formulas are an effort to prescribe a course of action for situations a leader may likely face. They are how-to strategies and tactics that attempt to plot each move, each step that a person in a leadership position should take to deal with a particular problem, situation, or concern.

Like an actor reading from a script or a dancer following the choreographed movements to a piece of music, these gurus lay out an essentially "managed" approach to leadership. The problem with this approach is that you cannot choreograph a leader's response to a wide range of human activity and organizational change. You cannot manage leadership as if it was some scientific calculation where adherence to formulas equals good leadership.

Good leaders recognize that leadership is an art, not a science, and as such, it cannot be managed or choreographed with predetermined step-by-step formulas for leaders to follow as they face the challenges of leadership. Good leaders look for approximately 75 percent solutions or chance of being right and then rely on their innate, instinctive leadership talent to fill in the gap. Put another way, good leaders know how to ad-lib or improvise, and they are at home being spontaneous and unrehearsed. The weight of a managed and controlled approach to leadership is both agonizing and tedious to a good leader. What's more, good leaders see the debilitating side effects of managed leadership from following formulas to deal with leadership challenges. These side effects include the following:

- hesitating to take action because of a desire to collect sufficient data to be 99 percent certain before moving forward
- accepting formulas as near guarantees of success, which promotes a false sense of certainty
- adhering to a structured step-by-step methodology, which unnecessarily constrains and controls good leaders
- avoiding taking risks by operating outside the steps of the sanctioned formulas

Bottom line: Good leaders do not lead by following predetermined formulas or choreographed steps. They follow the instincts of their own innate leadership talent and move forward to meet any leadership challenges.

8

GOOD LEADERS AND PARENTS HAVE SIMILAR GOALS FOR THEIR CHILDREN, EMPLOYEES, AND CITIZENS

All right-minded parents want their children to do better in life than they did. Good parents want their children to grow up healthier, better educated, more successful, and capable of being self-supporting and open-minded. Good parents will work long hours and make sacrifices to invest the time, caring, and money needed to ensure that their children have the support and resources they need to be successful in life and pursue their own aspirations. This level of parenting not only helps the individual child grow into a mature adult, but it also strengthens the family unit and contributes to the well-being of America.

Similarly, good business leaders see the wisdom of investing in their employees' individual and collective training and development.

Good leaders will ensure that their employees possess the support and resources needed to be successful in their jobs and to prepare them for higher-level assignments and challenges. Good leaders want their employees to succeed and take on additional levels of authority and responsibility. Good leaders sincerely care about their employees' welfare and understand that the success of their organizations is directly related to the success of their employees. Furthermore, good leaders recognize that one of their key responsibilities is to identify and develop the next generation of leaders.

From a national perspective, the president and Congress, as elected officials and leaders, should be motivated by a similar desire to invest in American citizens to ensure that our country will be better off than when these elected officials inherited it. The keystone of a national investment in American citizens is education. As Nelson Mandela said, "Education is the most powerful weapon which you can use to change the world." It is the great equalizer. Equal employment opportunity becomes a reality, because an education opens doors and affords all people the opportunity to compete on a more level playing field. Good leaders understand that ensuring access to an affordable education above the high school level must be one of America's highest priorities as a nation.

Parents, business leaders, and elected officials each have a responsibility and obligation to invest in their children, employees, and citizens and thereby pass on a better America to the next generation. *Each generation of Americans has a sacred obligation to improve our nation and leave it better off than we inherited it.* Good leaders know that we cannot remain a great nation, a great republic, if we are focused only on ourselves and our own pursuit of happiness. We must always be appreciative of the opportunities that America offers and give back and share our expertise and lessons learned with our children, employees, and citizens.

9

GOOD LEADERS UNDERSTAND THE INTERDEPENDENCE OF GOVERNMENT AND BUSINESS

The main goal of any business is to successfully compete in the marketplace and make a profit. These earnings are then used to pay the salaries and wages of the workforce, meet business expenses, and determine if a percentage of the profits should be reinvested in the business for expansion, which creates additional jobs. Vibrant and successful businesses are essential for a robust economy, which greatly contributes to sustaining a strong nation. Good leaders in both government and business recognize this fundamental and vital connection and understand that the government, through the laws it passes and the taxes it enacts, can create an economic environment conducive to business growth and profit making, or the government can suffocate new businesses and cripple corporations under a mountain of regulations. Even worse, government can do nothing and make no decisions, which can leave businesses uncertain about how to proceed with their plans to expand and hire additional workers.

Similarly, while business leaders want an unrestricted free-enterprise system to conduct their business and pursue profits, they must acknowledge their responsibilities as good stewards of their workforces, the environment, and thereby the nation. It's in the best interests of both government and business that the relationship between the two be grounded in the need for both to accept their obligations to our republic and its citizens first and foremost. Profits are a sign of businesses' good health, while informed and timely decision making is a sign of government's good health. Good leaders understand that both benefit from the acceptance of each other's role in maintaining a strong America.

However, too often we've witnessed chief executive officers (CEOs) leaving failing corporations or financial institutions and being rewarded with millions of dollars as they're walking out the door. These CEOs were concerned about themselves and not the businesses and institutions of which they were in charge. Some CEOs do not accept their responsibilities to their workforces, the environment, and the nation that gave them the free marketplace within which to conduct business. Their personal pursuit of power and profits condemned the organizations they ran into the ground to at least an uncertain future or a bankruptcy. Workers will lose portions of their salaries, many will be laid off, and retirement plans will be reduced or lost altogether while CEOs walk away with millions in lucrative severance packages.

In addition, we are witnessing the rapid expansion of a global marketplace where businesses are moving their operations outside America to foreign countries with the lowest corporate tax rates and cheapest labor. In this global marketplace, there is little recognition by many CEOs of their obligations to America and American workers. Jobs and dollars are sent oversees to finance and produce goods previously manufactured in America, while many CEOs turn a blind eye to the sweatshop working conditions in the foreign countries producing these goods.

Once again, the motive of many CEOs is profits over responsibilities, market share over their obligations to support a strong domestic economy and America. Capitalism does not give CEOs the right to do anything they want in any part of the world simply because they have the money and power to do just that. The all-encompassing quest for profits—no matter the cost to the environment, workers, and our nation—drives some CEOs to measure business success or failure by a single standard: profit. And when that happens, greed for more wealth than what is needed becomes simultaneously the motive and objective for too many CEOs. Good business leaders recognize and affirm their obligations as Americans to our republic.

As a nation we cannot remain strong and a force for good in the world unless we have a strong domestic economy. *While capitalism is clearly the appropriate engine upon which our economy and business enterprise should be conducted in an open marketplace, good leaders cannot allow irresponsible CEOs to turn this engine into a personal instrument for them to amass power and profits for their own enrichment.* Abraham Lincoln said, "These capitalists generally act harmoniously and in concert to fleece the people." Good business leaders understand that capitalism, left unchecked, will trend toward the creation of monopolies and conglomerates to reduce competition and maximize profits in the hands of a few, with little regard for its social and environmental responsibilities, thus disenfranchising millions of workers.

Theodore Roosevelt was very concerned about this and worked to bust up the monopolies of his time and ensure that the American workers had an opportunity to participate and prosper in the new economy. He worried that if the people were left out of the prosperity that capitalism brings, they would revolt. We need more CEOs like Bill Gates, who clearly recognize their social responsibility to give back a portion of their profits and wealth amassed through capitalism to improve the well-being of Americans and others. Responsible entrepreneurs can become a force to evolve into "capitalists with a conscience."

10

THE SOLITARY NATURE
OF LEADERSHIP

President Harry Truman had a sign on his desk that read, "The Buck Stops Here." As president, Truman recognized that he was ultimately responsible for the decisions he and his administration made. Likewise, individuals in leadership positions should have the same sign on their desks, because the message applies to all leaders at all levels. Truman's four words place a heavy burden and deep sense of responsibility on anyone who has authority over other people.

Once you accept a leadership position, you are no longer—to use an analogy—just a rider on a bus; you are now the driver of the bus, and there can be only one bus driver. The driver can ask the passengers for input on how to improve the bus or form a committee to determine the best route to take to their destination, but at the end of the day, the driver will be the one person responsible for the operation of the bus and the well-being of the people on the bus. The weight of leadership cannot be shared or delegated in any form or to anyone. This responsibility and accountability rest with the leader and the leader alone.

From team leader to president, the buck stops with each leader. Good leaders accept this and understand that the decisions they make can determine the success or failure of their mission and the individual and collective futures of their employees. Good leaders bear the weight of leadership, because they know that they have the innate leadership talent to effectively deal with the challenges of leadership. Good leaders will also ensure that their people have the tools, training, and support they need to succeed. And most importantly, they will deal with any person under their authority who is a conduct or performance problem; to do otherwise could jeopardize the mission and erode the people's trust in their leaders.

Being in command, being the one person with his or her hands on the steering wheel of the bus, will naturally cause a leader to feel separate or apart from the rest of the team. For good leaders, this weight of being responsible is balanced by the sheer exhilaration of being the leader, of doing what good leaders were born to do. Good leaders will embrace the responsibility of leadership and acknowledge the reality of being separate and yet inseparable from their teams. They understand and accept the solitary nature of command, of being the *one* in charge, of being the one person who is accountable and yet at the same time being an integral part of the team.

Poor leaders and especially new leaders must guard against being cut off and isolated from the team by becoming entranced and entrapped by the power of command and an inflated ego. If this occurs, then the leader will, in fact, become separate from the team and truly alone, and in that case the sign on a poor leader's desk will read, "The buck better not stop here," or "I will return when my people clean up all these bucks," or "I want the name of the person who sent this buck to me." As President Dwight Eisenhower once said, "Leadership consists of nothing but taking responsibility for everything that goes wrong and giving your subordinates credit for everything that goes well."

11

DEALING WITH THE INTOLERABLE BOSS

The overwhelming results of employee surveys consistently reflect that the number-one issue in the workplace is poor leadership or, more bluntly, an intolerable boss. Throughout my career of forty years in leadership positions and as a human resources director, I witnessed firsthand the demoralizing effects poor leaders have on their employees and the toxic environment they create every day for their workforces. Workers reluctantly come to work because they dread facing the reality of another day of dull assignments and working for an awful boss. Once at work, they are seldom engaged or committed to accomplishing their assigned work. And even more troubling, a sizable percentage of workers are completely disengaged and actually spreading discontent throughout the workforce.

The source of this worker discontentment is the intolerable boss who wreaks havoc in the office and on the shop floor every day. Estimates of $360 billion annually in lost productivity are evidence of the seriousness of the problem of workers who dislike or hate their jobs and boss.

To combat this situation, some businesses instituted an array of perks, from nap pods to massages, with limited success. Let's be clear—there is no amount of perks that will compensate for having to deal with an awful boss. These intolerable bosses can be divided into two main groups.

The first group epitomizes the title of *boss* and rules their work sites and the employees in them with an iron hand. These bosses typically make all the decisions and do not solicit input from their workers. They often use fear and intimidation to bully their employees to achieve the performance level and goals of the organization.

The second group can be described as do-nothing bosses. These bosses typically are procrastinators and want to preserve the status quo and will not make any decisions or allow any changes until they are 99 percent sure that the decision or change is the right one. Things get done on their work sites not because of them, but in spite of them.

Intolerable bosses act this way because they refuse to admit to themselves that they do not possess the level of leadership talent required to be an effective leader. They can manage work and issue orders, but that's not leadership. Additionally, employees are very reluctant to complain to higher-level managers about their heavy-handed bosses, because they fear retaliation, and they realize that higher-level managers rarely take any action to effectively deal with a poor leader. Consequently, employees just grin and bear it every workday, and they have little or no loyalty to the organization, its mission, and its goals. It's just about getting a paycheck for employees who work for an intolerable boss.

This debilitating scenario plays itself out in our government offices, businesses, and financial institutions and has negatively impacted employee morale, driven up turnover, and increased training costs. For an organization to be successful, its leadership must deal with the intolerable boss. To do so, we must understand that these intolerable bosses or poor leaders are products of the scientific approach to leadership, which has been the predominant methodology followed to create leaders for generations in America. Leadership gurus adopted this scientific process of discovery in an endeavor to define and measure human beings with the premise that anyone can be made into a leader.

Using science as a model, these gurus put successful leaders under the microscope to discover what traits, behaviors, and personality profiles make them successful, and then they compile these findings into formulas that, when followed, will replicate good leaders in mass. As a result, we continue to identify, select, train, and develop people for leadership positions using this fundamentally flawed premise that anyone can be made into a leader provided that they follow the leadership gurus' step-by-step formulas.

However, the solution to the problem of our disengaged workers and poor leaders is not more regimented and barren formulas; it's admitting that what we have been doing for generations to create good leaders has failed and we must move in a new direction, one where we regard leadership not as a commonplace skill that can be learned by anyone, but rather a recognized and prized innate talent that is critical to the success of America. *The most effective way to deal with intolerable bosses is to not make any more of them.* To do that, we must approach leadership as an art and focus our efforts on the identification and development of natural-born leaders who have the God-given gift of leadership that has been passed down in the form of DNA from biological parents.

Accordingly, once an intolerable boss is identified, senior management must remove that person from a leadership position and either utilize the individual in a nonleadership position or terminate the employment of that poor leader. If senior-level leaders are not prepared to take aggressive action, then the question is how many more employee surveys and reports will be needed to break free of the guru's pseudoscientific approach to leadership? At what percentage of workforce disengagement and job hatred will we finally see the need to change? How many more billions of dollars in lost productivity will have to occur before action is taken? How long will we continue to focus on the symptoms of poor leadership instead of the poor leadership itself?

All we need is the will to move in a different direction—one where we acknowledge the importance of innate leadership talent and realize that it doesn't come in a "prescription" from the leadership "gurus" who promised their personal brand of leadership elixir.

12

GOOD LEADERSHIP DOES NOT COME ATTACHED TO A DIPLOMA

As a nation we know that good leaders are needed in all sectors and levels of our society. The demand is great, and we've approached this need by creating leadership classes, workshops, and seminars designed to mass-produce good leaders. These training sessions have been built around the premise that everyone can be made into a leader. Government officials, corporate CEOs, small-business owners, and others in leadership positions have accepted this premise as fact. Each year training events are scheduled and booked as recently hired leaders and other leaders sign up to be shown the way to good leadership for all.

But there is a problem; this leadership training doesn't produce the results it claims. What typically happens is that after completing leadership training and the associated fanfare surrounding the presentation of certificates or diplomas, the newly trained and now gung-ho leaders go back to the daily routine at their work sites, and within a few weeks the class guidebook is buried on a shelf. And for the most part, everything goes back to the way it was prior to completing the training.

Good leaders, being natural-born leaders, will incorporate those aspects of the training they believe valuable into their daily practice while recognizing that there are no training events that will create good leaders. Leadership training and development are of little value if the people taking the training do not have the necessary level or degree of innate leadership talent.

Mark Twain once said, "Never try to teach a pig to sing; it wastes your time and it annoys the pig." This quote can easily apply to the inability to correct poor leadership through training. Poor leaders simply do not possess the innate know-how to lead, so they are unable to translate leadership training into action and reality at their work sites. Something is holding them back from becoming good leaders, and that something is a lack of innate leadership talent.

To reinvigorate the process, the organization sponsoring a particular guru leadership training event will often contract with another leadership "expert" in the hope that a different guru message will get through to the poor leaders, but it won't. The issue isn't the reputation of the instructor or the content of the training material. If a person does not have innate leadership talent, then it doesn't matter how much training, coaching, or inspirational encouragement a person gets; that person will never become a good leader. Training can enhance the talent already in a person, but no amount or type of leadership training can make a person into a good leader. You either have the needed leadership talent or you don't. You can either accept that reality or continue to be a leadership imposter. Understand that, if you choose the latter, your employees can see through your masquerade. *Leadership is not a thing that can be transferred from one person to another through training and a diploma; it is something that is a God-given talent that either you are born with or you're not.*

13

LEADERS CAN BENEFIT FROM THE US MARINES' "RULE OF THREE"

As a former US Army officer and a civilian supervisor of a 105-person organization, I've personally experienced the pressure and stress associated with working on multiple assignments with often competing resources, goals, and deadlines. After much study on this topic, the Marine Corps concluded that there is a clear connection between the number of objectives marines have to complete and the ability to accomplish those assignments, especially during active combat situations. The marines operate based on an underlying principle that war is chaos and they must learn to deal with the unexpected. They found that they needed maximum agility on the battlefield, and to do that it was necessary to reduce layered organizational structures, push more decision making down the chain of command, and limit the focus of marines to three objectives or goals to accomplish on any one mission. The marines determined that an individual's or unit's ability to successfully accomplish a mission is in jeopardy when more than three objectives are assigned.

This "Rule of Three" permeates how the marines strategize and structure for battle. For example, a corporal is in charge of a three-person fire team; a sergeant has three fire teams; a lieutenant has a platoon of three squads; and there are no more than three objectives designated for each assigned mission.

For government and business leaders, the leadership lesson to be learned from the Marine Corps' Rule of Three is that there is a limit to how much workers can handle and remain successful. That limit will vary by type of workload assigned, and like the marines, good businesses and government leaders must analyze their respective workloads and define the upper limits of the number of tasks that can be assigned for their particular circumstances. Senior leaders then need to agree on the top priorities that are crucial to the success of the organization, allocate the resources needed to successfully accomplish these priorities, and then aggressively drive the changes needed to achieve these priorities. As one priority is finalized, replace it with the next priority in order. When new procedures are required, they must be written in clear and concise terminology so that employees can understand them without need of a law degree. *It is the role of a good leader to drive the complexity out of an issue and frame it in its most basic terms.*

This may sound simple to do, but it is not. Businesses and government organizations routinely labor under a heavily layered organizational structure that is slow to respond and stifles discourse and innovation. Work is often assigned without allocating sufficient resources to complete the assignments within required deadlines. Employees are often not kept apprised of the organization's top priorities or when the priorities are modified or eliminated due to changes in our fast-changing world. And as a result, top-priority workload is mixed in with work of a lesser priority, thus losing the urgency for completion. Incorporating the marines' approach provides for a greater level of rigor, discipline, and sense of urgency on the part of the business and government communities that are designed to ensure that the objectives are achieved and the mission is accomplished.

14

TRYING YOUR BEST IS NOT GOOD ENOUGH

As a former cadet army officer in the Reserve Officer Training Corps, the training I received was designed to push me and my fellow cadets to the limit of our endurance, and it did. Carrying a heavy backpack and rifle for miles in forced-march conditions with summertime heat and humidity drained the energy out of us. And when we thought we couldn't go another step, the drill instructors acted like we were just out on a Sunday stroll and, with as uncaring an attitude as possible, ordered us to pick up the pace and continue to march. Every time I thought I couldn't continue, I somehow found the strength to keep going, and more importantly I began to believe that I could actually do this—that I could push myself and accomplish more than I ever thought possible if I was completely committed to the task at hand and believed in myself and fellow cadets to get the job done. I could do this. I have never forgotten the lessons in endurance, commitment, and self-confidence that I learned during my time in the US Army.

Subsequently, as a supervisor in several departments in the federal government, I attempted to apply the lessons learned in the army to my employees and to advise other supervisors as a human resources director. Too often I heard some employees say upon receiving an assignment and deadline that they would "try" to get the assignment done on time or that they'd do their "best" to get it done. Leadership often did not challenge these statements, and as a result, in a number of instances, the designated employees did not complete their assignments on schedule. While they gave reasons for their failure, good leaders know that the statements "I'll try hard to get it done" and "I'll do my best" are, in reality, employees giving notice that they lack the self-confidence and personal commitment to get the job done and on time. Good leaders recognize this and will work to improve their employees' ability to get the job done by staying engaged and committed to leading the way by working to build their employees' self-confidence and belief that individually and collectively they are able to accomplish more than they ever thought possible.

To be successful, leaders must believe and invest in their employees, and employees must believe in themselves and their leaders. Good leaders, like good drill instructors, know how hard to drive their employees so that they can stretch and grow more confident and committed. To create and maintain robust and competitive organizations, good leaders must strive to create a corporate environment and culture where leaders and employees make a commitment every day to get the job done no matter what. *Good leaders ensure that everyone realizes that there are no prizes for trying. In the end, life rewards those who do, not those who try.*

15

IT'S EASIER TO ASK FOR FORGIVENESS THAN TO ASK FOR PERMISSION

Poor leaders do not want to make a decision or start down a particular path unless they are personally convinced by the analysis of the available information and data that they have a 99 percent chance of making the right decision or going in the right direction. However, with the fast pace of change in the world today and the demanding deadlines to meet, waiting for the near-perfect solution prior to making a decision can hamper the ability of an organization to remain competitive and relevant. Supervisors who institute a strict methodology to be followed to generate a decision will quickly fall victim to their own rigid process. Inflexibility in leadership will soon turn into *leadership rigor mortis,* and a poor leader will often choose to do nothing rather than take the chance of making a bad decision.

Good leaders understand early on that the ability to weigh options by employing a flexible and collaborative form of decision making is essential for generating sound decisions. They do not need reams of data or a 99 percent chance of being right before they are willing to act. Typically, good leaders target a 75 percent chance of being right, and then they will take action and adjust on the move, relying on their innate leadership ability to guide and maneuver them. The problem is that these potential risk takers often work for a poor leader who feels more comfortable maintaining the status quo and is reluctant to make a decision and take action.

Consequently, good leaders are faced with the dilemma of seeing the need to act, of being willing to act, and of knowing how to act but realizing that the authority to act will not be forthcoming from poor higher-level leaders. In these situations, asking for permission to act is pointless and most likely will generate a negative response from these poor leaders that will restrict any independent action. For this reason, good leaders who strongly believe in the need to act for the best interests of the organization, its mission and customers, and the workers in it will often not wait indefinitely for the authority to take action from a poor leader, nor will they ask permission to act. General Norman Schwarzkopf, allied commander in the first Iraq war, said, "Do what is right, not what you think the higher headquarters wants or what you think will make you look good." The general is clearly laying out his criteria for taking an action that might not be approved by a higher headquarters.

Good leaders understand the risks associated with independent action and accept responsibility for any unauthorized actions. In those cases it's easier to ask for forgiveness and honestly explain your motives. If the unauthorized action taken is successful, then most likely all will be forgiven. But if the action results in failure, then a good leader must be prepared for and accept any repercussions from his or her actions. *In an organization with proactive and effective leadership, no one should have to ask for forgiveness after taking needed actions.*

16

COMPETITION AND COOPERATION: GOOD LEADERS RECOGNIZE THE NEED FOR BOTH

The history of mankind is one of intense competition between individuals, groups, and countries, with war being the most extreme form of competition. As human beings, we compete in everything we do, and we are each born with a unique set of physical and mental attributes and innate talents that individualize and separate us as we compete with others, for example, for control of a particular toy with a sibling, for superiority in a wrestling match, for the attention of an attractive person, for employment, for recognition and promotions at work, for being a member of the US Olympics team, for winning the World Series or the Super Bowl, for wealth, for power, or for military superiority. The list is endless.

While some forms of competition can be divisive and violent, good leaders recognize that many other forms of competition can help people discover their own unique set of innate talents. We can learn through our successes and failures about whom we are and what we are really good at. And most importantly, we can learn how to deal with failure, because we most certainly will experience more failure than success in our lives. Competition encourages us to constantly push ourselves and raise the bar for our own performance. Good leaders know that the more they can match their employees to the jobs and careers in which they are talented, the more likely they will be outstanding employees, because they will be doing what they were born to do.

Cooperation is equally important to competition, because it acts as a force multiplier. Good leaders know that when people act together as a team, they are truly greater than the sum of their parts or individual team members. We are capable of great accomplishments, especially if we take advantage of the various talents that each person brings to a team. Plus, the knowledge that each person possesses can be shared so that the entire team can grow and become more multiskilled and valued members of an organization.

Often cooperation and competition overlap—for instance, in sports, where the cooperative need to pull together to support the best interests of the team override the individual competiveness of each person to be the best at a particular position. In sports the game itself and the team are more important than anyone's individual accomplishments. There are some people who favor the hard-hearted aspect of competition and say, "No one helped me, so why should I help anyone else?" But if we are honest with ourselves, we have all been helped and supported at some time, and it is vital that we reach out in a cooperative spirit and give back wherever we can.

We must leave this nation better off than we inherited it. Good leaders understand that democracy and America are more important than anyone's individual accomplishments. There are also those who want to make everyone a winner and give them all a trophy just for participating. Competition is a reality, and giving everyone a trophy when they didn't earn it will not insulate anyone from the cold hard realities of competition. We must embrace competition and strive for greater cooperation. There is an old African proverb that deals with this topic: "If you want to go fast, go alone. If you want to go far, go with others." To sustain a strong republic, we must go forward together.

17

BEING A GOOD LEADER IS MUCH MORE THAN AN EIGHT-TO-FIVE JOB

For both first-time and longtime leaders, there are several fundamental realities regarding employees' expectations of their leaders that must be understood and accepted to be good leaders. Employees expect their leaders to

- always be engaged in their organization's business and daily operation,
- be approachable to answer their questions or provide advice,
- always be ready to take on the issues and problems of the day,
- represent their interests at meetings and briefings,
- leave their personal troubles at home,

- be objective and open-minded when presented with different opinions or alternative suggestions, and
- be impartial and not show any favoritism within the workforce.

Based on this, good leaders need to recognize that employees' expectations of anyone in a leadership position are extremely high, and they will demand their attention. Good leaders will embrace these realities and respect the views of their employees. Poor leaders will be defensive and push back. Good leaders understand that the continued employment and careers of their employees depend on the investment in the training and development of their workforces to effectively handle today's operations, while preparing workers to deal with tomorrow's challenges. Progressive and forward-thinking leaders have a responsibility to ensure that their organizations and their workforces remain relevant and competitive. Good leaders work tirelessly to get the job done, recognizing that their success is directly related to having trained, motivated, and capable workforces. Employees want their leaders to understand and champion their interests. Workforces that are led by poor leaders know that their employment, careers, and reputations are in jeopardy, and they live every day with a high degree of uncertainty about what will happen to them tomorrow. Will they have jobs? Good leaders' expectations of themselves are that they must be "on the job," constantly working to ensure the success of their organizations and employees. That hard reality is the immense responsibility demanded of all good leaders twenty-four hours a day, seven days a week. *Being a leader isn't a job; it's a calling.*

18

TEAM SYNERGY CHALLENGED BY WORK-FROM-HOME PROGRAMS

The basic unit and building block in the workplace is the team, which is typically composed of a team leader and team members who are physically located together and collectively possess the requisite skills to be able to accomplish assigned tasks. As any team leader with innate leadership talent knows, creating and maintaining a team requires the ability to shape and forge a group of people with diverse backgrounds and perspectives into a productive and dynamic team. This process starts with leaders' selecting the right people as team members, investing in their training and development, providing them with regular feedback, acting as their role models, and explaining the interrelationship among the team members and the need for cooperation and mutual support to ensure that the team is successful.

Good leaders understand that these activities will build synergy within their teams, where each person is seen as vital to the teams' overall expertise, capability, and success. As the team works together, it will evolve its own unique identity, its own team chemistry. Good team leaders will build on this synergy and chemistry to create a sense of team esprit de corps. And good leaders will instill in their teams that taking care of their customers with superb service is the reason for the teams' existence. Once in operation, a team's performance can be impacted if there are changes in the team's composition, especially if the change is the team leader.

These changes will affect the team's synergy and chemistry, and team leaders must stay engaged as the team works to find a new identity. The increased efforts to implement work-from-home programs will be a huge challenge for leaders to deal with, as they must manage the impact on the synergy and chemistry of their teams. It is significantly more difficult to forge a strong team when the team is not physically together. A common workplace brings people together and fosters a connection and commitment to each other and the organization, which is lost when working at home. Good leaders understand that, as human beings, we are fundamentally social beings and have a strong desire to interact with each other, and the workplace provides a venue for this interaction. Technological advances to create virtual teams can accomplish work assignments, but they cannot satisfy our primal need for companionship and social interaction.

Good leaders know that the teams' focus must always remain on their customers, and any changes to the team and how it operates must be aimed at improving customer service and not just on implementing the "program of the month." What's more, employees view working from home as a benefit or "perk," which should be available to all employees in an organization. However, the type of work in which many organizations are engaged cannot be accomplished from home, and consequently, working from home is often restricted to certain job functions and the individuals assigned these duties. These restrictions create a feeling of being a second-class employee among those employees who are restricted from participating because of the nature of the work they perform. *If a leader cannot offer a perceived benefit to all employees, then it should not be offered to anyone.*

19

GOOD LEADERS HAVE THE "RIGHT STUFF"

The "Right Stuff" is a term coined by Tom Wolfe in his book *The Right Stuff*, which describes the challenges faced by American test pilots and early astronauts as they pushed to break the sound barrier and rocket to outer space. It deals with the undefinable makeup and character of these pioneering individuals, enabling them to successfully deal with the dangers and complexities of their professions.

I believe that the phrase "Right Stuff" also applies to leaders who have innate leadership talent, which is likewise undefinable and critical for their success. Good leaders have the "Right Leadership Stuff," and "Stuff" is the best way to describe the intangible art of leadership. Good leaders defy definition and labels. They just seem to have a natural gift for leading, a sixth sense of how to be a leader even without being in a leadership position. Leaders with the right stuff are born to lead; it's what they are best suited to do, what they were meant to do. Leaders with the right stuff project the proper degree of self-confidence and boldness without succumbing to conceit and arrogance.

When leaders have the right stuff, they draw upon an internal reservoir of talent that they tap into to deal with the challenges of leadership. They recognize that whatever success they experience as a leader is because of the leadership talent or gift with which they were born, and without that gift (or "stuff") they would not be effective leaders. This realization humbles good leaders. Rank and reward have no appeal to a leader with the right stuff. A bloated ego cannot survive inside a good leader. Leaders with the right stuff always put the best interests of their workers and mission above their own. *Possessing the right leadership stuff, a leader inherits the calling and duty to take the gift of leadership selflessly.*

20

SUCCESSION PLANNING: A CRITICAL ASPECT OF GOOD LEADERSHIP

Succession planning is the process of identifying qualified candidates for key positions well before the current incumbents vacate the positions, in order to minimize or eliminate any gap in filling these positions. The mistake that many organizations make is that they don't start doing succession planning until someone in a key position declares that he or she will be leaving the organization. Even if the person leaving gives one to two months' notice prior to his or her departure, that is not enough time to adequately conduct succession planning. The senior leadership of an organization should meet regularly to review their options for filling key positions. Senior leaders need to make succession planning a part of their daily routine by continually observing the people in their organization for the behavior, expertise, and insight that indicate someone with the ability to progress into leadership or other key positions.

Discussions will typically center on whether to hire individuals from outside the organization or from within. If the senior leadership frequently hires individuals from the outside, they are sending a strong message to their employees that either no one is ready to be placed into a higher-level position or there is no one in the organization that the senior leaders want in these higher-level positions—not now, not ever. Both situations are troublesome and reflect poorly on leadership for allowing these situations to occur and negatively impact the organization. The following actions can be taken to improve the succession planning process:

- Start now. Don't wait until someone has announced that he or she is leaving.
- Develop an initial list of the organization's key positions.
- Share the list with your workforce, and explain the need for succession planning.
- Solicit names of anyone interested in receiving developmental assignments to be competitive and qualified for future key positions. Don't screen out anyone at this initial stage.
- Meet with the interested employees, and explain how you plan to proceed.
- Conduct applicable formal classroom training.
- Provide developmental on-the-job assignments.
- Provide regular feedback to the participants regarding their performance.

Following these tasks will ensure that the organization will have internal candidates available and competitive for placement in its key positions when needed. *Good leaders understand that developing their workforces by investing in their collective and individual futures builds a mutual sense of loyalty and commitment by the leadership and employees toward each other. Such mutual commitment ensures organizational success and continuity.*

21

GOOD LEADERS RISE ABOVE ADVERSITY AND BAD BREAKS

Leaders have to deal with any and all adversity and bad breaks that impact them and the people they lead. That's part of what leaders do and are expected to do. When misfortune does strike, good leaders will move to quickly identify the source of the problem and implement either an immediate fix or develop a plan of action to deal with the situation over a longer term. In either case, good leaders will find the time to make an informed decision by soliciting input from as many of their employees as possible given any time constraints. If the problem demands an immediate fix and there is no time for collaboration, then good leaders will not hesitate to make the needed decision and then ensure that their employees are informed of the decision and the plan of action, and that the need for immediate action negated any collaboration.

The important point here is that good leaders need to create an environment and culture that value an inclusive and collaborative approach to handling adversity and decision making. Doing so will unify leadership and employees into a cohesive force that will be able to collectively rise above any adversities. Ultimately, it's in everyone's best interests to work together to find sound solutions and make collaborative decisions.

Poor leaders, on the other hand, will not be comfortable with such a culture of collaboration, because it will be seen as a constraint on their personal power as "the boss" to make the decisions. Since poor leaders typically want to maintain the status quo, no one wants to be the first to inform the boss of a problem, for fear that the poor leader will "shoot" the messenger, and consequently, by the time a problem is brought to the attention of the boss, it is often already at a crisis mode. And without a culture of collaboration, poor leaders will simply make reactionary decisions without consulting anyone outside their inner circle of confidants. The workforce will eventually be informed of the decision as fait accompli.

Furthermore, employees watch how their leaders personally react to adversity and bad breaks. They want leaders who don't overreact to situations and make everything into a crisis when, in fact, it is not. And they want leaders who can remain calm when confronted by difficult problems. Good leaders recognize that they must live up to their employees' expectations, and good employees must understand that even with collaboration and a strong relationship with their leaders, good leaders can still make some bad decisions and take erroneous actions. *Leaders should be measured and judged on their body of work over time and not on one instance of a bad choice or mistake.*

22

GEORGE WASHINGTON: A PROFILE OF INNATE LEADERSHIP TALENT

George Washington once said regarding leadership, "Remember that it is the actions, and not the commission, that make the officer, and that there is more expected from him, than the title." Washington was clearly making the point that just because a person is commissioned as an officer, that doesn't automatically make that person a good leader. What makes a good leader is not the title or rank, but rather the actions that the leader takes every day to ensure the well-being of the troops under the leader's command.

As commander of the American Army, Washington demonstrated a deep commitment to his troops, and he was always concerned for their morale and welfare above his own. He recognized that he was not just commander in chief; he was also "father in chief" of the men in his army. Washington knew that the troops under his command expected nothing less from him and that he needed to be more than just a title of commander. He had to display a very high level of innate leadership talent required to hold his inexperienced colonial army together and do battle with the British who at that time were the world's superpower. Through the many highs and lows of the American Revolution, he provided the innate leadership and resolve necessary to win independence.

Washington also said regarding the critical nature of leadership, "An army of asses led by a lion is vastly superior to an army of lions led by an ass." This statement shows that Washington believed that it is absolutely critical that only individuals with a high degree of leadership talent be placed in command. With the proper leadership, even an army of asses can be molded into a fighting force.

However, an army in the hands of a person who does not possess leadership talent will be ineffective no matter how trained, experienced, and ready for battle the troops are. Leadership at all levels is critical, but it is especially vital at the topmost commander or senior executive position, because this is the one position that is responsible for creating the culture and direction for an organization. Washington always took leadership seriously and used his personal leadership talent to lead our new nation to victory on the battlefield and as president.

23

GOOD LEADERSHIP IS THE PREREQUISITE FOR SUCCESS

Good leadership is the prerequisite and foundation of successful small businesses, large corporations, public institutions, military commands, governments, and nations. When good leadership exists within these entities, especially in the top executives or senior leaders, they will be vibrant, robust, and characterized as leaders who are

- motivated to ensure a positive legacy for the people they lead and not for their own personal desire for power and wealth;
- concerned about the greater good and development of their employees and citizens;
- critical of current processes and encourage innovation and initiative;

- focused on results, productivity, and the belief that together we can always do better; and
- driven to remain relevant and competitive by embracing change in an ever-changing world.

To accomplish these things, good leaders must have, in addition to a deep desire and commitment to be a leader, the innate leadership talent that is needed to be a good leader. This talent is the hallmark of natural-born leaders, and when organizations and countries are led by leaders who possess this innate leadership talent, they will flourish at all levels.

Natural-born leaders can lead regardless of the situations or circumstances. They can overcome rigid chains of command, oppressive organization structures, burdensome regulations and operating procedures, and employee and citizen apathy. Good leaders break down barriers to success and inspire their people with a sense of urgency and commitment to strive for a better tomorrow, always placing the common good over personal rank and reward. Natural-born leaders are easy to recognize but difficult to define. They come from every segment of society and apply the art of leadership, often ignoring the accepted or traditional path. Instead, they rely on an inner sixth sense or instinct to drive them forward. They possess the God-given gift of leadership that is transmitted through DNA. To ensure continued success for this great nation and the well-being of each American, we must stop trying to make everyone into a leader and instead finds ways to identify and develop natural-born leaders. As I've said in *Leadership DNA*, "No nation can become great or stay great without great leadership."

24

GOOD LEADERS WILL CONFRONT DIFFICULT ISSUES

Good leaders rely on their personal awareness of their own innate leadership talent to know when to engage in an issue, situation, or crisis. They seem to possess a sixth sense about how long to assess and analyze a matter and when to move forward and deal with it. Good leaders are quite comfortable with knowing when to apply the necessary level of leadership to a situation, and at the same time they reflect a sense of urgency to deal with the issues at hand. Good leaders speak openly and honestly regarding difficult issues and the inevitable changes that will come their way. They understand that problems do not get better with age and that it's best to acknowledge the problem openly and truthfully, deal with it, and move forward.

The act of standing up and expressing hard realities regarding difficult and emotionally charged situations demonstrates good leadership. Because of this, good leaders will develop over time consistent work ethics and leadership standards that are predictable and can be relied upon by their workforces. Workers know where they stand with good leaders. When they see their leaders stand up and take a stance for doing the right thing, it reinforces the bond between leaders and their workforces. *From reliability comes trust; from trust comes everything else. Standing up and being counted on is a simple act, but it symbolizes the essence of good leadership.*

Successful organizations have within them good leaders and responsible workforces that come together to form a partnership of mutual respect and commitment to each other. Good leaders establish formal mechanisms to ensure that their workforces have the means and opportunity to express their opinions. And good leaders will pay close attention to what their workforces are saying and incorporate that information into their decision making.

Poor leaders, on the other hand, are much less concerned with taking action. They are more interested in maintaining their position of importance and superiority in the organization. However, when it's time to be counted, poor leaders will often shrink from the responsibility of having to take action to deal with difficult situations and crises.

25

GOOD LEADERS UTILIZE
THE WHAT-IF EXERCISE
IN PLANNING

Leaders need to be able to see what is going to happen before it happens. This does not mean that leaders must be clairvoyant or psychic and be able to predict the future. Rather, good leaders understand that the key ingredient in the planning process is conducting a rigorous what-if exercise. Before taking any action, good leaders will ask the searching question, "What if we do this?" There will be an array of responses and options to that question, and each answer must in turn be thought through and played out by repeating the same question, "What if we do this?"

If the planning process is to be successful, it must proceed with collaboration with others in the organization. Good leaders know that conducting collective what-if inquiries will bring into focus a range of actions that can be taken and the strengths and weaknesses of each. Armed with this information, good leaders will be able to predict with a higher degree of probability the available courses of action that can be taken and their likely outcomes. The end result will be a level of assurance that if we take a particular action, then this reaction will happen. Consequently, this process will allow leaders, by the choices they make, to better "see" what is going to happen before it happens, to be able to get out in front of issues and establish direction and policy for the organization on a wide range of issues.

The best time to perform this exercise is before any crisis or situation arises that requires action. Once a crisis has occurred, the what-if exercise can still be effective, but it will be tied to and impacted by the current crisis, such as the performance or conduct of a particular person or failure to follow a procedure. This becomes a complicating factor that will often reduce the range of available actions. For example, a small-business owner rents space in a building for himself and his two managers, two clerical staff, a foreman, and fifteen automotive repairers. The owner of the building gives this new tenant three parking spaces next to the building for their use. The next morning the company's outstanding foreman starts parking his personal car in one of these parking spaces without asking for permission. In this scenario, the business owner just lost the opportunity to develop a plan for these three parking spaces before anyone started to park in them. Now the behavior of the foreman will become the threshold issue, and the what-ifs will revolve around the foreman's actions and reactions to the use of the parking spaces. Good leaders recognize that for the what-if exercise to be effective, it must start as soon as possible for a particular course of action to avoid the "foreman" impact.

26

THE DOUBLE-EDGED SWORD
OF EMPLOYEE RECOGNITION

Recognizing employees for a job well done can be a powerful motivator for the persons receiving the recognition and for those who witness the presentation of the recognition. At the same time, employee recognition can also be one of the most divisive and demoralizing events to impact an organization and the people in it, especially if the recognition includes awarding money.

Recognition is typically given to an individual or a group that accomplishes something above and beyond what would normally be expected. The controversy with recognition centers on the process for determining who gets recognition and why. Quite frequently the individuals receiving the recognition and the justification for the recognition are not supported by the other employees. This situation can quickly turn a time of celebration for those being recognized into a deep resentment over the process for determining who should receive the recognition. Employees feel that their supervisors too often do not know what is actually happening on a daily basis in the office or on the shop floor to be able to determine who has earned recognition.

Consequently, for recognition to be an effective tool to award superior performance, good leaders must understand the importance of recognizing the right people for the right reasons and the negative impact that getting it wrong can have on the workforce. The following elements outline actions that can be taken to maximize the positives of employee recognition programs and policies:

- Leaders typically witness firsthand only a small percentage of the performance of their employees. What is noteworthy for official recognition of an individual one day may not be justified for that same employee over a longer period of time for a variety of reasons. Good leaders will ensure that they have a sufficient sample of each person's performance to warrant recognition and that there are no disciplinary actions pending for any potential recipients. If there are, recognition should be placed in abeyance for those individuals until their cases are finalized.

- Team members work together to accomplish their assigned daily workload. Over time if a team's collective performance level warrants recognition, all team members should receive the same recognition provided that there are only small variances in performance by each team member. If, however, some team members do not contribute as much as the others due to an extended illness, being a trainee, or poor performance, then a good leader will investigate these situations to determine the best course of action, and the amount of recognition should be lowered or eliminated, as appropriate, for those team members. *Nothing aggravates employees more than when they see the low performers receiving the same recognition as the high performers.*

- Good leaders will ensure that team members selected for special assignments or projects are drawn from all interested teams without any prescreening or favoritism. These types of special tasks typically give the selected employees increased exposure to upper-level leaders or other key personnel, which often brings with the assignment a greater chance of recognition. If an award is recommended for the performance of those individuals working on the special assignment, good leaders will then determine if any recognition is also warranted for those other team members who absorbed their teammates' regular workload while they worked on the special assignment. This is an extremely important point that is often missed in recognition programs. Leaders see the contributions made by those who completed the special assignment but frequently overlook the people who provided the support. In such a situation, a higher form of recognition can be given to those directly assigned the special project, and a lesser form of recognition can be given to those in support. The key here is that good leaders will take the time to determine everyone involved with this special project and the extent of that involvement. The workforce will appreciate a leader who takes the time to get this right.

- For employees who occupy a one-of-a-kind position, the duties lend themselves to greater interplay with an array of higher-level leaders or action officers at a headquarters or company office complex. As a result, it's easier to produce the justification for recognition of these individuals. To ensure fairness, good leaders will make certain that the criteria for recognition of one-of-a-kind positions are comparable to the criteria for the organization's frontline work teams.

- Good leaders will make maximum use of nonmonetary forms of recognition that recognize the employees of an entire organization for their hard work, such as holding an employee appreciation day, leadership buying everyone pizza for lunch, or presenting workers with inexpensive gift cards for gas or groceries, to name a few. These low-cost high-return forms of recognition for all employees improve morale and provide a sense of comradery and belonging to an office or corporate family. *Good leaders will always understand that the most important form of employee recognition is for leaders to sincerely say thank you often and out loud.*

In general, it is imperative that organizations have recognition programs and procedures to ensure that deserving individuals and groups receive appropriate recognition when warranted. Employee perceptions regarding the fairness of these procedures are critical to having an effective program. Given this, good leaders will discuss their recognition programs with their employees and solicit feedback prior to implementation. The goal here is for the right person or group to receive the right form of recognition while always remembering that even good leaders can't please everyone when it comes to recognition and awards.

27

EMPLOYEES WHO ASSESS THEIR LEADERSHIP SKILLS WILL COMPARE THEMSELVES WITH THE WORST LEADERS, NOT THE BEST

In most career fields the lines of progression typically go from trainee or apprentice through several advanced levels or pay grades to eventually a technical expert or master craftsman. Once employees attain these highest nonleadership grades, they then must decide if they want to move from performing technical or craftsman work and apply for leadership positions, such as team leader or foreman. Good leaders know that employees desiring to move from nonleadership positions to leadership positions need to do honest self-analyses to determine their respective motives for wanting to be leaders and whether or not they have the innate leadership talent to be good leaders.

Regarding motive, if the main reason for wanting to be in a leadership position is to obtain an increase in salary and personal power, then that person will never be a good leader, because to be a good leader one must be selfless and put employees first and their well-being above one's personal interests. Regarding a personal assessment of leadership skills, the problem here is that an organization's leaders are not all natural-born leaders. Quite the opposite is actually the case, and an organization's employees who are applying for leadership positions are very aware of the fact that good leaders are in the minority.

Consequently, employees who want the increase in salary and power will compare their perceived leadership skills to the worst leaders in an organization, not the best leaders. This occurs because organizations typically do not effectively deal with their poor leaders. Too often the senior leaders allow poor leaders to remain in place while they say they are working to improve the organization's leadership. However, these poor leaders serve as indicators of the subpar leadership that the organization is, in reality, willing to accept. Therefore, employees deciding if they should apply for leadership positions regrettably do inadequate self-assessments and simply say to themselves, "I can be as good a leader as that person," referring to one of the poor leaders in the organization. Employees will judge the quality of an organization's overall leadership by its weakest links, which are individuals in leadership positions who have demonstrated that they shouldn't be leaders. These poor leaders must be aggressively dealt with whenever and wherever they are identified, because to do otherwise will further erode the quality of leaders in the organization.

Employees need to see that their leaders will be held accountable for a clear set of responsibilities and expectations so that potential applicants for leadership positions will understand that the organization is doing everything in its power to obtain the best leaders. To accomplish this, senior leaders should be continually assessing their leadership team to ensure that the leadership performance bar is raised high to make certain that it will no longer be business as usual for the organization's leaders. Now potential applicants for leadership positions will have to compare themselves to a higher standard of leadership talent.

Some organizations' senior leaders have decided to just wait until a poor leader leaves the organization altogether, and then they will attempt to do a better job selecting replacements in the hopes of improving the quality of its leaders. This is a mistake, because these senior leaders are now relying on leadership turnover to solve their leadership performance problems, which it won't, because most organizations are populated by numerous poor leaders. *Waiting for turnover within an organization's leadership ranks is not an effective way of dealing with a poor leadership problem. Senior leaders must own this problem and work to reduce and eliminate poor leaders in their organizations.*

28

THE IMPORTANCE OF EMPLOYEE ORIENTATIONS, ESPECIALLY FOR NEW EMPLOYEES

Conducting new employee orientations is one of the most critically important events for good leaders. These orientations are the opportunity for the leaders in an organization to explain to each new hire the organization's structure, mission, customers, and values. Most importantly, they show each new employee how their assigned duties and responsibilities fit into the organization as a whole. Good leaders understand that new employees want to know that what they are doing will contribute to the success of the organization. This gives people a sense of belonging from day one and a feeling that they are an important piece of the organization's operation.

Leaders should also use this event to go over available career paths within the organization and any training and development open to employees to demonstrate that the organization is willing to invest in its employees' futures. These orientations provide a forum for leaders to explain any probationary periods and individual performance and conduct expectations to ensure that each employee is fully aware of these requirements from day one.

New employees should additionally be introduced to the other members of their assigned team or working group, with an explanation of the new employee's role on the team or group. Ideally, these initial introductions should also include the next higher-level leader in the organization who can reinforce certain key topics discussed during the orientation.

For employees already part of the organization, good leaders will utilize a modified version of the new employee orientation to orient those who are transferred or promoted to a different set of duties and responsibilities within the organization. This reinforces that sense of belonging and commitment of the organization to the employee and ensures that the employee understands the organization's expectations. Good leaders also will follow up with the new hires or newly promoted employees within normally forty-five days to ensure that they are progressing satisfactorily. Good leaders know that a quality orientation will greatly contribute to the smooth transition of employees into their new duties.

In an organization with poor leadership, the new employee orientation is normally comprised of a handshake by the poor leader, small talk with the new employee, and a quick welcome to the organization, and then the leader rushes off to a meeting. The task for actually orienting the new employee is too often delegated by poor leaders to senior employees in nonleadership positions. This is a bad practice, because while the senior employee can discuss the "mechanics" of how things work in the organization, only a good leader can convey how important the new employee is to the organization. *A leader who does not recognize the importance of investing the time to personally conduct a first-class employee orientation is clearly a poor leader who will negatively impact the growth of both the newly assigned employee and the organization itself.*

29

A KEY PIECE OF
GOOD LEADERSHIP
IS REENGINEERING
WORK PROCESSES

Good leaders realize that they have a responsibility and obligation to provide their workforces with well-designed work processes and procedures that facilitate the accomplishment of assigned work and aid in the growth of employee skills and expertise. To achieve this, good leaders will

- define customer expectations, production goals, quality requirements, and performance measures;
- identify the organization's key work processes;
- streamline the tasks within each process;
- organize around these key processes to maximize productivity; and

- examine the potential to reduce organizational layers and improve internal communications.

To accomplish these elements of reengineering, good leaders will acknowledge that they must incorporate their employees into these reengineering activities. The employees know how things really work in the office or on the shop floor; they know where current procedures are working and where they are not. From this understanding of what works and what doesn't, employees can offer valuable perspectives on what processes and procedures need to be created, updated, or eliminated. In addition, good leaders realize that the reengineering process can be an opportunity for an organization's leadership and employees to collaborate on improving the organization's processes and thereby unit production and customer satisfaction. What's more, incorporating employees into the reengineering efforts will clearly demonstrate that the organization values their employees and that this is tangible proof of the leadership's understanding that for the organization to be successful, the leaders and workers must have a common purpose and understanding of the way forward.

Unfortunately, the reality is that too many employees work within organizational structures and processes that for the most part were created by poor leaders and managers with little or no input from their workers. Poor leaders view any real collaboration with their employees as an attempt to reduce their own personal authority. Poor leaders argue that most employees do not see or care about the big picture. In reality, employees only want to use the reengineering process as an opportunity to get rid of some of their duties and make their jobs easier.

While that may be a motive for some employees, it's not for the vast majority of employees. Employees want their organizations to be successful so that they can retain their jobs and participate in the organization's success through potential salary increases, bonuses, or improvements to benefits packages. Always remember that an organization's employees are a reflection of what the leadership models every day in their words, actions, and attitude. *If a leader cannot trust an employee to do the right thing for the organization, then the fault lies with the leader.*

30

THE NEGATIVE IMPACT OF A MICROMANAGER ON AN ORGANIZATION AND ITS EMPLOYEES

Micromanagers are individuals who believe that they must personally manage all aspects of their team's work to ensure that their employees' assignments are properly completed within established deadlines. Micromanagers have a deep-seated need to control things and are typically convinced that if they want something done right, then they have to do it themselves. Micromanagers assign the work to their employees and then almost immediately establish meeting times to "look over their shoulders" to ensure themselves that each team member is following their directions on how to properly complete their assignments. This creates a very stressful work environment where what you do and how you do it are being closely controlled and monitored.

This situation of extreme scrutiny will inevitably lead to employee stress, mistakes, and errors. Once mistakes are made or deadlines are not met, micromanagers will typically say that they knew this would happen. Now they have to personally clean up the mess because the failure reflects back on them and they can't trust anyone else to do it as well as they can. What these managers don't realize is that they've created a workplace environment that is built on the premise that if micromanagers are not constantly managing the work, the employees are incapable of getting the job done, as required.

Such a perception becomes a self-fulfilling prophecy where micromanagers expect that their employees are going to fail and the employees sense the lack of trust, lose their self-confidence, and actually begin to fail; this only reinforces micromanagers' beliefs that their employees will not complete their assignments as required. A sense of distrust and apprehension permeates the workforce and creates unnecessary stress on the employees. Johann Wolfgang von Goethe, a German writer and statesman, made a point that is applicable here: "The way you see people is the way you treat them, and the way you treat them is what they become." Micromanagers see their employees as prone to fail if they do not receive the controls and oversight needed to accomplish their work assignments. Faced with such a perception, employees will gradually cease to expect anything from themselves and become reluctant to take any action without the approval of their supervisor. *Innovation, initiative, and risk taking are casualties of micromanagement.*

Good leaders understand that as human beings, no one is perfect, and we all make mistakes or fail to complete assignments at one time or another. Micromanagers compensate for this "imperfect human factor" through tight controls and frequent oversight. In contrast, good leaders see their employees as critically important assets in the accomplishment of work assignments. They see each assignment as an opportunity to coach their employees on how to successfully complete these assignments and understand that organizational success is directly related to each employee's personal success. The more employees can become successful in the workplace, the more there is individual growth and a greater degree of commitment to the organization. Instead of tight controls, good leaders foster an environment that builds self-confidence and trust in the workplace by doing the following regarding completing assigned work:

- Meet with each employee to review the requirements of the assignment to ensure that there is agreement on what needs done and when. It is vital that each employee fully understand the scope of their assignment before proceeding.
- Schedule periodic reviews to coach, not control.
- Immediately discuss any change in the assignment with the employee, and clarify how this change may modify the original assignment requirements.
- Apply the right amount of coaching to employees who are in jeopardy of not completing their assignments. Overreacting and smothering an employee with too much "help" can be detrimental to the employee.

With both good leaders and micromanagers, the endgame is to have completed work assignments done on time, every time. What's different is their approach. Micromanagers control and monitor their employees' progress out of fear that the assignments will not get completed on time and that this will reflect poorly on their leadership ability. Good leaders, in contrast, work to develop their employees so that they are competent, self-confident, and capable of getting the job done by utilizing coaching, not an abundance of controls. Micromanagers are focused on the completion of the assignment; good leaders are focused on the development and growth of the employees working the assignments.

Micromanagers can be successful in the short term but at a very high price to the competence and self-confidence of their subordinates. *Good leaders say what needs to be done, not how to do it. They know that determining the "how" challenges employees to demonstrate the innovation, initiative, and risk taking needed to complete assignments and ensure individual and organizational success in the long term.*

31

DEALING WITH THE PROBLEM EMPLOYEE

Good leaders recognize that when dealing with poor performance or misconduct, there is often a deep-seated inertia and reluctance by poor leaders to take action to effectively deal with problem employees for a variety of reasons:

- Poor leaders know that their employees' poor performance or misconduct can reflect back on them as the individuals who originally hired or selected the now-problem employees.

- Poor leaders also know that failing employees can reflect badly on them and on the organization if the problem employees were not provided with the appropriate training, tools, guidelines, and support needed to become good employees.

- Firing problem employees increases turnover costs associated with training replacements and temporarily filling the vacancies created by the dismissed employees.

- Poor leaders typically shy away from conflict and do not like to confront problem employees, and when they do attempt to counsel poor employees, it is with the hope that once the poor performance or misconduct is presented to the employee, this initial confrontation will be enough to improve the performance or stop the inappropriate behavior. It rarely does.

- An employee's poor performance or misconduct was identified early in the process, but the poor leader took little action, and what action was taken was not properly documented. Poor leaders who allow poor performance or misconduct to continue over an extended period of time will eventually become so disgusted with this situation and the problem employee that the poor leader will want the problem employee dismissed for the latest wrongdoing regardless of the seriousness of the offense.

- As time passes with no action taken, poor leaders often move the poor performer's work to another employee, because the poor performer is not getting his or her assigned work completed. This nonaction and movement of work aggravate the workforce, because they recognize that they're being directed to take on the work of someone who is not carrying an equal workload. The other workers will resent both the poor performer and the poor leader for allowing this to happen. For misconduct cases, poor leaders have a tendency to say that the behavior is not that bad and just attempt to put up with the misconduct.

For these reasons, little is done with the problem employee until the poor performance or misconduct becomes so chronic and unavoidable that something must be done to correct the situation. To maintain their credibility with the workforce, good leaders know they must

- operate with a sense of urgency to deal with poor performance and misconduct, because the workforce is watching how leadership handles these situations and especially how long the poor performance or misconduct are permitted to go on without corrective action;
- ensure that a problem employee does not receive recognition simply because he or she is part of a team that earns such recognition;
- refocus the workforce on their mission and away from the status of the poor employees, and the only way to do that is to deal with the problem employees now; and
- review the actions or lack thereof of poor leaders regarding how they handle problem employees.

Good leaders have a responsibility to ensure that the leadership of an organization is populated with other good leaders who know how to coach for success and ensure that all employees are treated equally and provided the tools and support to be successful. By so doing, good leaders create an environment for a productive and committed workforce where employees know what is expected of them and that swift action will be taken if any employee or leader fails to carry out the responsibilities of their respective jobs.

PART 2

GOVERNMENT AND POLITICS

32

MEDIOCRE LEADERSHIP HAS BECOME THE NEW NORMAL

How many times have you gone into the voting booth and voted for the lesser of two evils? How many times did you wish you had the option to vote "None of the Above" and force both the Republicans and Democrats to put people on the ballots who actually possess leadership talent? How many times have you witnessed one politically engineered fiscal crisis after another? How many times have you watched as the White House and Congress allowed partisan politics to gridlock our government? How many times have corporate CEOs run their companies into the ground and then desert their workforces to face corporate bankruptcy? How many times have these same CEOs left unscathed with severance packages worth millions of dollars? As Americans, we collectively yearn for good leaders to emerge who clearly possess the leadership ability needed to unify America and create a climate for life, liberty, and the pursuit of happiness for all.

But we've been disappointed and disillusioned for so long that we've come to accept this lack of good leadership "as is." We've consciously or subconsciously lowered the bar regarding what we expect as citizens and are willing to accept from our leaders in government, business, finance, and so forth. We have allowed poor leaders to occupy key leadership positions without possessing the required innate leadership talent to be effective leaders. This has resulted in an epidemic of poor leadership in both the public and private sectors of America. Regrettably, many of our leaders have placed their own personal or political party's interests above the best interests of the nation. And what is painfully clear is that our acceptance of mediocre leadership has become the new normal.

However, if we do not have good leaders in our society, then as a people and a nation we will eventually become less and less competitive and influential throughout the world. Abraham Lincoln said, "America will never be destroyed from the outside. If we falter and lose our freedoms it will be because we destroyed ourselves." To correct our leadership problem, we must identify and develop natural-born leaders who have innate leadership talent and stop electing, appointing, and hiring mediocre or poor leaders. We must not accept mediocre leaders in our leadership positions as the new normal. We the people must raise our expectations of our leaders and clearly communicate to them that great leadership is what we expect, and as Americans we will accept nothing less.

33

COMPROMISE: A BRIDGE TO AGREEMENT OR A SIGN OF WEAKNESS

When our Founding Fathers came together to write the Declaration of Independence and US Constitution, they represented colonies and peoples that had diverse needs and different points of view. To form this country, they recognized that they were not going to get everything they wanted; if their efforts were going to be successful, they had to compromise. And this need for compromise was hardwired into the divided form of government upon which they agreed. Power is shared among the executive, legislative, and judicial branches of government with no branch superior to the other two. What's more, the legislative branch was further subdivided into the House of Representatives and the Senate. When you add in the Bill of Rights, our Founding Fathers went to great lengths to create an

American system of government that demanded debate and most importantly a willingness to compromise to get something done. They purposely built a government structure of multiple layers of checks and balances at the national and state levels that were designed to discourage and prevent anyone from attempting to usurp power.

Even with this constrained governmental structure, they were able to form a new democratic government during a period of rebellion, war, and immense uncertainty throughout the colonies. The ability to compromise demonstrated a person's political skill and statesmanship as our country struggled to survive.

Fast-forward to today, and Americans face a new set of issues. But today we seem to no longer value compromise and statesmanship. Today too many of our politicians and leaders see compromise as a weakness to be exploited and used to defeat those with opposing points of view. Politicians championing the far-right and far-left agendas battle it out, trying to convince the American public that the other side is not just wrong; they're completely wrong and detrimental to America. Meaningful debate and open discourse have been lost in parliamentary procedures designed to stymie and control deliberations. Savvy politicians are masterfully using our divided form of government to either get the outcomes they want or grind everything to a halt.

In either case, they are undermining the very essence of American government. Statesmanship and mutual respect have been replaced by crass politicians and partisan politics. A willingness to compromise by moderate lawmakers targets them for defeat by lobbyists, radicals, and political donors at the next election. For any real patriot, compromise is not a sign of weakness. *America needs leaders who are selfless and put the interests of the people and the nation above political parties, elections, liberalism, and conservatism. Most importantly, these leaders must understand that this country was built on compromise and a sacred recognition of differing points of view where no one person, party, or ideology has a monopoly on the truth and the right path for America.*

34

YOU CAN'T LEAD LOOKING
IN THE REARVIEW MIRROR

As a nation and a people we must take a lesson from nature and realize that there are only two options for any living being: either move forward and grow, or stand still and decay. Good leadership is about moving forward. A good leader's focus must be on the road ahead and the challenges around every new corner in this twenty-first century. In doing so we cannot, however, ignore the past or we shall be condemned to repeat it. At the same time, our leaders in government, business, finance, and so forth cannot chart a course for America by constantly trying to steer this country by looking in the rearview mirror.

For centuries, the distance and difference between past, present, and future were not that great. Little changed in how people lived from generation to generation. The past, present, and future all ran together in a slow parade of sameness, minimal invention, and relative predictability. This was all changed with the advent of the industrial and technological revolutions. The advances in science and technology have brought enormous changes to our society at an ever-increasing pace.

Looking in the rearview mirror for the lessons of the past has become less and less relevant, as we now face issues and problems on a scale never encountered by the civilizations and peoples of the past. The distances and differences between past, present, and future are growing wider and more pronounced with every new generation. As a result, America needs leaders who can lead during times of massive change, who can move forward under a banner of flexibility and agility, no longer steadfastly and too often blindly bound to a specific ideology such as liberalism or conservatism or to a specific political party. At the end of the day, we need leaders who can make the tough, forward-thinking decisions that will lead us into an uncertain and transforming future. And most importantly, we need a citizenry that will accept nothing less from its leaders and themselves. As good leaders move the country forward, our prime directive must be that we will never allow democracy to perish in this new world.

35

RUGGED INDIVIDUALISM VERSUS COMMUNITY OUTREACH: COMPETING PHILOSOPHIES IN AMERICA

As stated in *Leadership DNA*, two fundamentally different philosophies exist in America that shape how we approach life in general and government in particular.

The first philosophy is rugged individualism and dates back to the first settlers who came to America and started small communities in the New World with little support. These were strong-willed individuals who valued their freedom and independence and for the most part were against invasive governments and laws. They faced terrible hardships as they settled along the eastern coast and then journeyed west as they went from colonists to pioneers. They learned that if they were going to survive, they had to depend on themselves and a close-knit family structure. As stated in *Leadership*

DNA, Theodore Roosevelt summed up rugged individualism when he said, "The first requisite of a good citizen in this republic of ours is that he shall be able to pull his own weight." Roosevelt also said further on this point, "The worst lesson that can be taught to a man is to rely upon others and to whine over his sufferings."

Benjamin Franklin also spoke on this rugged individualism topic: "In my youth I traveled much and I observed in different countries, that the more public provisions were made for the poor, the less they provided for themselves, and of course became poorer. And on the contrary, the less was done for them, the more they did for themselves and became richer." Generally, the Republican Party has inherited the rugged individualism and a small-government philosophy.

Community outreach is the other philosophy, and it formed around a broader sense of communal kinship and cooperation for group protection and survival. As towns and cities sprang up, there was a growing need for more government, social structure, and recognition of a moral requirement to provide some degree of public assistance to the less fortunate members of society. The Democratic Party has assumed the community outreach viewpoint of more social safety-net programs and an expanded role for government to provide assistance to those in need.

These two often-conflicting philosophies or "personalities" of Americans have clashed over how we should collectively deal with a wide range of local and national issues. We can readily witness how the political positions taken by Republican and Democratic proposals reflect these competing philosophies that have manifested themselves throughout our history. Both have their particular strengths and weaknesses, and when either is taken to an extreme, animosity and gridlock occur, with the protagonists willing to fight to their political deaths for their respective philosophies.

Good leaders recognize the need to embrace both philosophies and approaches to govern effectively. They understand that the community outreach or more liberal approach is initially necessary to ensure that Americans have the assistance they need to utilize safety nets and support programs and, most importantly, access to a good education.

Regarding education, Thomas Jefferson said, "Educate and inform the whole mass of the people. They are the only sure reliance for the preservation of our liberty." Jefferson clearly recognized that an educated America is the key to becoming a vibrant democratic nation.

With a more liberal philosophy initially in place to provide people a solid first step in life, good leaders will then be in a position to implement a more follow-on conservative philosophy that expects each person to become a responsible adult accountable for their actions, obtain employment, reduce their reliance on government programs, and engage in the political and economic opportunities available to an American citizen.

As President Ronald Reagan said, "Welfare's purpose should be to eliminate, as far as possible, the need for its own existence." In this way both philosophies have a place in America and can thrive side by side with equal importance for our republic and appeal to all Americans to put the best interests of the nation above philosophical differences. *As Americans, we all contain the seeds of both rugged individualism and community outreach, and the course for America will be defined by the way good leaders harness the positives of these differing philosophies and reject their extremes.*

36

GOOD LEADERSHIP ENSURES THAT AMERICA'S BEST DAYS ARE ALWAYS TODAY AND TOMORROW

Too often, you hear some people saying that America's best days are behind her, that we don't seem to have the resolve to deal with the big issues anymore, that we lost what once made us great. Throughout our history, each generation of Americans has had to make nation-shaping decisions that continue to form our collective values and culture. Our forefathers authored the Declaration of Independence, the US Constitution, and the Bill of Rights, proclaiming the rule of law and that all men are created equal, but they left slavery in place, were silent on the status of Native Americans, and denied women the right to vote in this new republic. The slavery nightmare was finally abolished with the issuance of the Emancipation Proclamation, the ratification of the

Thirteenth Amendment, and the deaths of 620,000 Americans in our bloody Civil War. Women protested and eventually won the right to vote. Pioneers settled this huge country and joined east and west with railroads while at the same time decimating Native Americans in the process. Americans fought for freedom in two world wars, and yet we had segregated military units.

We are a people capable of great achievement and compassion, along with great destruction and cruelty. Despite this mixed record, Americans possess a deep sense of fair play, tolerance, and national pride as a nation and for the past 230-plus years have fought to find their democratic identity in a world of tyrants and dictators, where oppressed people throughout the world look to America for hope and freedom.

America needs leaders who recognize that democracy can be full of missteps and growing pains as this nation works to adhere to the principles laid down by our Founding Fathers. Benjamin Franklin was asked after he participated in creating the US Constitution, "What have you wrought?" Franklin replied, ". . . a Republic, if you can keep it." This is the great challenge and historical obligation that are passed down to the leaders and citizens of every generation as a sacred trust to come together to protect this republic of the people, by the people, and for the people. Good leaders understand and accept this sacred trust to always put the interests of the nation first, above any personal agendas or political ideologies. Mistakes have been made, and man's inhumanity to man will manifest itself from time to time in America as we strive to do the right thing. We need good leaders in all segments of our society who understand our collective frailties and at the same time recognize a boundless American spirit that is capable of accomplishing anything. Good leaders know that America's best days are not behind her. Each generation of Americans must pass the torch of freedom to the next generation to ensure that our republic does not fail.

37

THE POOR, THE MIDDLE CLASS, AND THE RICH IN CLASSLESS AMERICA

The Declaration of Independence and US Constitution made it clear that all men are created equal, which meant that there would be no classes of people in the new American republic. Despite this we constantly hear our politicians refer to the poor, middle class, and rich in their speeches, political campaigns, and proposed policy initiatives targeting one or more of these groups, which I will refer to as pseudo classes. While a person can move from one pseudo class to another due to individual initiative, money, invention, higher education, and so forth, labeling somebody as being part of a certain class of people brings with that label a whole host of perceptions and misperceptions about the people in that pseudo class.

These categories and labels only serve to further divide Americans into different camps. We don't need to treat the people in these pseudo classes as if they fit some murky caricature. They do not. Our modern-day pseudo classes are primarily built upon wealth or the lack thereof and, more specifically, the government-defined yearly income thresholds for the poverty level and richest Americans.

However, there are no clear definitions for membership in any of these three. Being poor is not a character flaw. Being rich does not require an apology. Everything is fluid, and in today's America there are no fences or bloodlines imprisoning a person in one particular group. A quality education is the prime ticket that can increase salary, self-esteem, and upward movement. As one nation, good leaders understand that we do not need any rallying cries from politicians attempting to pit one pseudo class against another or lay blame for America's financial problems on a particular faction. Good leaders recognize that we are all citizens of this great republic and need to work together to improve the well-being and livelihood of all Americans.

This is the land of opportunity, and people need to recognize that, appreciate it, and take advantage of it. Where people can pull their own weight, we should expect them to. Where they physically or mentally cannot, then we need the community outreach to provide a safety net to assist them. And most importantly, we must stop referring to people as members of some ill-defined class. There are no classes in America by definition of our own Constitution and Declaration of Independence.

38

GOOD LEADERS WILL NOT ALLOW AMERICA TO BE HELD HOSTAGE TO POLITICAL AGENDAS

Good leaders negotiate; politicians posture. America is drowning in a sea of posturing with little leadership as we face self-inflicted crises. Our nation lacks the consistently effective leadership needed to deal with partisan politics and our exploding debt, both of which threaten to choke the future out of our country. Politicians are fond of saying that they must follow their principles and develop a course of action to get the country going in their own definition of the *right direction*. In the meantime, they often believe it's better to do nothing, because to do otherwise would send the country off in the *wrong direction*.

Good leaders recognize that there are real problems with this nonaction approach:

- America has an educated and diverse citizenry, and no single politician or political party can speak for all Americans or even most of us.
- Given that we live today with constant domestic and global change, we cannot as a nation afford to just do nothing every time some group of politicians decides that they are going to gridlock the government and society until they get their way.
- Corporations, small businesses, and financial institutions need some degree of certainty in the marketplace to formulate their own plans to react to government policies. Doing nothing hurts our economy. Good leaders cannot allow politicians who are more concerned about their own party's interests than that of the nation to hold America hostage to their radical agenda and vision of a perfect republic.

Compromise is the only answer, but compromise has come to be seen by politicians as abandonment of principle. To be pragmatic is seen as unprincipled. Quite the contrary, compromise is the engine that good leaders use to drive movement, and once moving, they adjust their course and speed, as needed. *Good leaders do not wait for the perfect plan or moment to do something. They take action and, by so doing, do not allow America to be held hostage to anything or anyone.*

39

THE SELF-RIGHTEOUS MINORITY

Elections don't seem to settle anything anymore. One political party wins an election, and regardless of the margin of victory, the other party circles the wagons and prepares to use every legislative protocol and administrative procedure (of which there are an endless number) to impede, block, and grind to a halt the entire governing process. At the beginning of each new term of office, the election winners believe that they have a mandate from the American people who just elected them to propose, debate, and pass bills and take any other actions needed to deal with the issues raised in the campaign. And most importantly, there is an expectation that this should be done within a reasonable time frame.

A government, such as ours, that is of the people, by the people, and for the people must move forward in the direction in which *we the people* voted to go. Regardless of which party won the presidency and majority of seats in the Congress, the people have spoken through the election process, and both parties should recognize that public mandate and resulting obligation to do what is necessary to accomplish the people's agenda.

However, it doesn't work that way. What actually occurs is that the party that suffers the greatest losses in the last election immediately begins to analyze the polling and voting results to develop a plan of action to win the next election. Typically, the minority party decides that the best way for them to win the next election is by thwarting every effort by the majority party to pass any bills or solve any of the major issues facing the nation. Their goal is to ensure that there's a do-nothing White House or Congress to run against in the next election. The justification for this approach can be summed up in the words "the self-righteous minority." The party in the minority sees itself as the one with the right message, the message that reflects how the people *should* have voted, how they *should* think, and how the country *should* be governed. They see themselves as the only ones who are loyal to the principles of the US Constitution, and consequently, they know better than the majority of Americans regarding how to govern this country.

To maintain a strong republic, good leaders understand that we, as a government and a people, must honor election results and work together to reach compromises to keep our country moving forward; doing nothing until the next election is not an option. The world in which we live is rapidly changing, and it will not allow us years of inaction to position political parties to win the next election. Good leaders know that whether we like it or not, America is the leader of the free world, and that world depends on the United States for leadership. If we fail to provide it, then nature abhors a vacuum and some other country, some other people, will step up and fill the leadership void.

Both Democrats and Republicans equally need to recognize that we must move forward and reach compromises on the current set of problems that require action and then prepare ourselves for the next round of challenges in this new century. Doing otherwise places the interests of a political party over the people's agenda and above the interests of the nation. Good leaders recognize that America does not need a self-righteous minority or a domineering majority. We need compromise and a recognition that, as Thomas Jefferson said, "We in America do not have government by the majority. We have government by the majority who participate."

40

A WARNING FROM GEORGE WASHINGTON ABOUT POLITICAL PARTIES

In his Farewell Address on September 17, 1796, George Washington said, "However [political parties] may now and then answer popular ends, they are likely in the course of time and things, to become potent engines, by which cunning, ambitious, and unprincipled men will be enabled to subvert the power of the people and to usurp for themselves the reins of government, destroying afterwards the very engines which have lifted them to unjust dominion." These words were spoken by the father of our country and our first president as he was leaving office. This was a clear warning regarding the harm political parties and power-hungry politicians can have on our government. The framers of the Constitution, of which Washington was a member, detested political parties and believed they would divide the nation into competing factions and promote their own party's interests over the interests of the entire nation.

Washington's words and warning are especially important because he turned down attempts to make him the king of our new nation. He said that "I didn't fight George III [king of England] to become George I [king of America]." After serving eight years as president, he upheld the US Constitution and transferred power to John Adams, our elected second president. Washington's words and actions ensured that our young country would remain a republic and not turn into a kingdom.

Fast-forward to the early twenty-first century, and we see that Washington's and our Founding Fathers' concerns and predictions regarding political parties have come to pass. We have political parties continuing to split Americans into factions. Large sums of monies come pouring in from political action groups all in an attempt to buy political influence and push a particular agenda that is good for only certain segments of American citizens. Campaign promises are forgotten a few months after being elected. Politically engineered dysfunction and gridlock have become tactics used by each party to advance its own interests.

We the people need natural-born leaders in the White House and in Congress who are concerned with ensuring the well-being of our country over the need to push personal and party agendas. We need our elected representatives to be statesmen instead of self-absorbed politicians. We need the White House and Congress to come together for the benefit of the nation and demonstrate real leadership and deal with their irreconcilable differences. We need Republicans and Democrats to stop the crass rhetoric and character assassination in the media and go work out their differences like adults. We need our representatives to realize that we are all Americans first and foremost. And we must heed the warnings of Washington and the other Founding Fathers regarding the negative impact political parties can have on America. Mark Twain said it best: "Politicians are like diapers; they need to be changed often and for the same reason."

CONCLUSION

These forty essays provide a sampling of the wide range of issues, situations, and challenges that people in leadership positions face every day. How well public and private sector leaders deal with these circumstances will assist in determining if they have innate leadership talent. As I've said before, the only way to know if a person has leadership talent is to place that person into a leadership position and observe the individual's performance when faced with the pressures and demands of being a leader. At the same time, good leaders recognize that they need to continually step back and review their words and actions to ensure that they are using their God-given talents for the benefit of those under their leadership or command. *Good leaders understand that the leadership talent they possess is a DNA gift and not something they obtained and developed on their own. Accordingly, a deep sense of humility is a hallmark of good leaders.*

Good leaders are able to overcome roadblocks and adversities by applying their unique innate leadership talent. They understand the philosophical and real-world differences between the science of leadership and the art of leadership. Good leaders embrace a reality where instinct, a sixth sense, and listening to your gut are much more important than pseudoscientific formulas pushing a one-size-fits-all approach to leadership. The leadership gurus claim to have developed their step-by-step formulas for leadership success. They say that, if followed, these formulas can make anyone into a leader. Good leaders, on the other hand, recognize that each person is unique, and with the art of leadership comes multiple approaches to dealing with real-life issues. As unique individuals, there is no one way to lead.

Good leaders know that if a person has innate leadership talent, then that talent cannot be ignored or silenced; it will find a way to express itself. In addition, good leaders foster an environment and culture that emphasize collaboration and the inclusion of various points of view. When good leaders are in command, they identify problem areas and will set about to deal with them. As a result, good leaders bring a sense of hope that things will be better, that by pulling together, the organization will function more efficiently and effectively, and the opinions of the workforce and citizens matter and will receive full consideration. All of this is especially important at the national, state, and local government levels, where we hope as citizens we've elected good leaders to lead our nation—leaders who can use their innate leadership talents to spread a message of hope and confidence about the future and provide our nation with the leadership it so desperately needs.

APPENDIX

For ease of reference, I've compiled the quotes used in this book along with my personal insights and comments, which are marked by italicized text:

You can put a person in a leadership position, but you can't put leadership in the person.

The science of leadership argues incorrectly that leaders can be made by simply following step-by-step formulas and that leadership is a commonplace skill that can be learned by anyone. However, the art of leadership argues that leaders are born as unique individuals with a set of unique talents. The leadership gurus' equation (personal desire + commitment + leadership training = real leadership) is fundamentally flawed because it does not account for innate leadership talent and the uniqueness of each person. Once individual talent is factored in, then the valid equation will read: desire + commitment + leadership training + innate leadership talent = real leadership.

Quote: Thomas Jefferson said, "The Creator has not thought proper to mark those on the forehead who are of the stuff to make good generals."

Quote: Colin Powell, former chairman of the Joint Chiefs of Staff and secretary of state, said, "That's what you really have to look for in life, something that you like and something that you think you're pretty good at. And if you can put these two things together, then you're on the right track and just drive on."

Quote: Johann Wolfgang von Goethe, a German statesman and writer, also said regarding this topic, "The person born with a talent they are meant to use will find their greatest happiness in using it."

Quote: Abraham Lincoln said, "America will never be destroyed from the outside. If we falter and lose our freedoms it will be because we destroyed ourselves."

America needs leaders who are selfless and put the interests of the people and the nation above political parties, elections, liberalism, and conservatism. Most importantly, these leaders must understand that this country was built on compromise and a sacred recognition of differing points of view where no one person, party, or ideology has a monopoly on the truth and the right path for America.

Quote: As stated in *Leadership DNA*, Theodore Roosevelt summed up rugged individualism when he said, "The first requisite of a good citizen in this republic of ours is that he shall be able to pull his own weight."

Quote: Roosevelt also said further on this point, "The worst lesson that can be taught to a man is to rely upon others and to whine over his sufferings."

Quote: Benjamin Franklin also spoke on this rugged individualism topic: "In my youth I traveled much and I observed in different countries, that the more public provisions were made for the poor, the less they provided for themselves, and of course became poorer. And on the contrary, the less was done for them, the more they did for themselves and became richer."

Quote: Thomas Jefferson said, "Educate and inform the whole mass of the people. They are the only sure reliance for the preservation of our liberty."

Quote: Ronald Reagan said, "Welfare's purpose should be to eliminate, as far as possible, the need for its own existence."

As Americans, we all contain the seeds of both rugged individualism and community outreach, and the course for America will be defined by the way good leaders harness the positives of these differing philosophies and reject their extremes.

Quote: Benjamin Franklin was asked after he participated in creating the US Constitution, "What have you wrought?" Franklin replied, "... a Republic, if you can keep it."

Good leaders don't just make decisions; they make decisions better.

Good leaders do not wait for the perfect plan or moment to do something. They take action and, by so doing, do not allow America to be held hostage to anything or anyone.

When negotiating, winning cannot become more important than agreeing.

A workforce is a reflection of its leadership, or, put another way, leadership gets the workforce it deserves.

Quote: John F. Kennedy once said, "Change is the law of life. And those who look only to the past or present are certain to miss the future."

Quote: And his brother Robert F. Kennedy said, "There are those who look at things the way they are and ask why ... I dream of things that never were, and ask why not."

Poor leaders work within the current system of facts; good leaders change the system and create new facts, new realities. Poor leaders remain at rest; good leaders realize that if you rest you rust.

Bottom line: Good leaders do not lead by following predetermined formulas or choreographed steps. They follow the instincts of their own innate leadership talent and move forward to meet any leadership challenges.

Quote: Nelson Mandela said, "Education is the most powerful weapon which you can use to change the world."

Each generation of Americans has a sacred obligation to improve our nation and leave it better off than we inherited it.

While capitalism is clearly the appropriate engine upon which our economy and business enterprise should be conducted in an open marketplace, good leaders cannot allow irresponsible CEOs to turn this engine into a personal instrument for them to amass power and profits for their own enrichment.

Quote: Abraham Lincoln said, "These capitalists generally act harmoniously and in concert to fleece the people."

Quote: We need compromise and a recognition that, as Thomas Jefferson said, "We in America do not have government by the majority. We have government by the majority who participate."

Quote: As President Dwight Eisenhower once said, "Leadership consists of nothing but taking responsibility for everything that goes wrong and giving your subordinates credit for everything that goes well."

The most effective way to deal with intolerable bosses is to not make any more of them.

All we need is the will to move in a different direction—one where we acknowledge the importance of innate leadership talent and realize that it doesn't come in a "prescription" from the leadership "gurus" who promised their personal brand of leadership elixir.

Quote: Mark Twain once said, "Never try to teach a pig to sing; it wastes your time and it annoys the pig."

Leadership is not a thing that can be transferred from one person to another through training and a diploma; it is something that is a God-given talent that either you are born with or you're not.

It is the role of a good leader to drive the complexity out of an issue and frame it in its most basic terms.

Good leaders ensure that everyone realizes that there are no prizes for trying. In the end, life rewards those who do, not those who try.

Quote: General Norman Schwarzkopf, allied commander in the first Iraq war, said, "Do what is right, not what you think the higher headquarters wants or what you think will make you look good."

In an organization with proactive and effective leadership, no one should have to ask for forgiveness for taking needed actions.

Quote: There is an old African proverb that deals with this topic: "If you want to go fast, go alone. If you want to go far, go with others."

Being a leader isn't a job; it's a calling.

If a leader cannot offer a perceived benefit to all employees, then it should not be offered to anyone.

Possessing the right leadership stuff, a leader inherits the calling and duty to take the gift of leadership selflessly.

Good leaders understand that developing their workforces by investing in their collective and individual futures builds a mutual sense of loyalty and commitment by the leadership and employees toward each other. Such mutual commitment ensures organizational success and continuity.

Leaders should be measured and judged on their body of work over time and not on one instance of a bad choice or mistake.

Quote: In his Farewell Address on September 17, 1796, George Washington said, "However [political parties] may now and then answer popular ends, they are likely in the course of time and things, to become potent engines, by which cunning, ambitious, and unprincipled men will be enabled to subvert the power of the people and to usurp for themselves the reins of government, destroying afterwards the very engines which have lifted them to unjust dominion."

Quote: George Washington said that "I didn't fight George III [king of England] to become George I [king of America]."

Quote: Mark Twain said it best: "Politicians are like diapers; they need to be changed often and for the same reason."

Quote: George Washington once said regarding leadership, "Remember that it is the actions, and not the commission, that make the officer, and that there is more expected from him, than the title."

Quote: Washington also said regarding the critical nature of leadership, "An army of asses led by a lion is vastly superior to an army of lions led by an ass."

Natural-born leaders can lead regardless of the situations or circumstances.

As I've said in Leadership DNA, *"No nation can become great or stay great without great leadership."*

From reliability comes trust; from trust comes everything else. Standing up and being counted on is a simple act, but it symbolizes the essence of good leadership.

Nothing aggravates employees more than when they see the low performers receiving the same recognition as the high performers.

Good leaders will always understand that the most important form of employee recognition is for leaders to sincerely say thank you often and out loud.

Waiting for turnover within an organization's leadership ranks is not an effective way of dealing with a poor leadership problem. Senior leaders must own this problem and work to reduce and eliminate poor leaders in their organizations.

A leader who does not recognize the importance of investing the time to personally conduct a first-class employee orientation is clearly a poor leader who will negatively impact the growth of both the newly assigned employee and the organization itself.

If a leader cannot trust an employee to do the right thing for the organization, then the fault lies with the leader.

Quote: Johann Wolfgang von Goethe, a German writer and statesman, made a point that is applicable here: "The way you see people is the way you treat them, and the way you treat them is what they become."

Innovation, initiative, and risk taking are casualties of micromanagement.

Good leaders say what needs to be done, not how to do it. They know that determining the "how" challenges employees to demonstrate the innovation, initiative, and risk taking needed to complete assignments and ensure individual and organizational success in the long term.

Good leaders understand that the leadership talent they possess is a DNA gift and not something they obtained and developed on their own. Accordingly, a deep sense of humility is a hallmark of good leaders.

BIBLIOGRAPHY

All quotes in this book were found in BrainyQuotes.com or Notable-Quotes.com unless otherwise notated.

Thomas Jefferson. FamousQuotesandSayings. Accessed July 12, 2015. http://www.quotes.net/quote/41502.

Powell, Colin. "America's Premier Soldier-Statesman." Academy of Achievement Interview, May 23, 1998. Accessed July 12, 2015.

Benjamin Franklin Quotes. Thinkexist. http://Thinkexist.com/quotation/a republic-if-you-can-keep-it/580171. Accessed July 12, 2015.

Norman Schwarzkopf: "10 quotes on Leadership and war." Forbes. Accessed July 12, 2015. http://www.forbes.com/sites/kevinkruse/2012/12/27/norman-schwarzkopf-quotes/.

The Best 72 African Wise Proverbs and Inspiring Quotes. AFRITORIAL. Accessed July 9, 2015. http://afritorial.com/the-best-72-african-wise-proverbs/.

Theodore Roosevelt Quotes. Brilliant.Life.Quotes. http://www.brilliantlifequotes.com/inspirational/theodore-roosevelt-quotes/. Accessed July 12, 2015.

Mark Twain Quotes. refspace. Accessed July 12, 2015. http:www.refspace.com/quotes/Mark Twain/Q2727.

Mark Twain Quotes about Politics, Freedom, and Patriotism. Brilliant.Life.Quotes. Accessed July 12, 2015. http:www.brilliantlifequotes.com/inspirational/mark-twain/Accesed July 12, 2015.

INDEX

A

adversity, 73–74

America

best days, 121–22

class in, 123–24

consensus and, 13

economy and, 33

education and, 30

leadership vacuum in, 1, 3, 129

philosophies in, 117–19, 139

See also government

B

bad breaks, 73–74

business

government and, 31–32

C

capitalism, 33–34, 140

change, 20–22, 78, 115–16

chief executive officers (CEOs)

and profits over

responsibilities, 33

and severance packages, 32

children, investing in, 30

citizens, investing in, 30

coaching, 101

collaboration, 73–74, 96, 136

community outreach, 117–19, 139

competition, 57–59

compromise, 5, 14–16, 111–13, 126, 128–29, 138

consensus, 13–14

cooperation, 57–59

D

decision making, 13, 24, 54, 74

democracy, 14, 59, 116, 122

Democratic Party, 109, 118

E

education, 30, 119, 123–24, 140
Eisenhower, Dwight, 37, 141
employees
    investing in, 29–30, 52, 63,
        71, 92
    opinions of, 80
    orientations for, 91–92
    poor performance of, 103–5
    recognition for, 83–86, 105
    reengineering process and, 96
    self-assessment of leadership
        qualities, 88
    transfers and promotions, 92

F

facts, 21–22
fair-market system, 5
Franklin, Benjamin, 118, 122, 139
free-market system, 5

G

Gates, Bill, 34
global marketplace, 32–33
Goethe, Johann Wolfgang von, 10,
    100, 138, 144
government
    business and, 31–32
    checks and balances, 112
    compromise and, 111–13,
        126, 128
    gridlock and, 109, 118, 126, 132
    mediocre leadership and, 109–10
    political agendas, 125
    political parties and, 126–27

    self-righteous minority in,
        127–28
    statesmanship, 112
    taking action and, 127
    See also democracy
gridlock, 109, 118, 126, 132

H

hierarchy, 23
hire from the outside, 70

I

initiative, 19, 24–25, 77, 100
innate talent, 2–4, 11, 28, 36, 41–
    42, 57–58, 78–79, 88, 135–37
innovation, 19, 24–25, 48, 77, 144
intolerable boss, 39–42

J

Jefferson, Thomas, 3, 119, 129,
    138–39, 141

K

Kennedy, John F., 21, 140
Kennedy, Robert F., 21, 140

L

leadership
    art vs. science, 2–3, 28, 41,
        135, 137
    difficult issues and, 79
    dissatisfaction about, 2
    employee expectations, 61–62, 74
    formulas and, 1–3, 11, 27–28,
        41, 126
    identifying natural-born leaders,
        3–4, 42, 78, 110

innate talent and, 2–4, 11, 28,
     36, 41–42, 57–58, 78–79, 88,
     135–37
managed vs. spontaneous, 28
mediocre leadership, 109–10
moving forward, 115–16
poor leadership, 41–42, 53–54,
     62, 74, 88–89, 93, 96
responsibility of, 34–37, 54
selflessless and, 88, 138
solitary nature of, 35–36
success and, 77–78
taking action, 55, 70
teams and, 63–64
training and, 1–3, 27, 43–44
vacuum, 1, 3, 129
Lincoln, Abraham, 33, 110, 138, 141

M

Mandela, Nelson, 30, 140
micromanagers, 99–102
middle ground, 5
middle management, 25
misconduct, employee, 103–5

N

natural-born leaders. See innate
     talent
negotiations, 15–17

O

Olympics, 10
organizational structure, 25, 47
orientations, new employee, 91–92

P

parenting, 29
political agendas, 125–26
political parties, 126–29
politics. See government
Powell, Colin, 9, 138
priorities, 48–49
procedures, 48, 95–96
promotions, employee, 92
pseudo classes, 123–24

R

Reagan, Ronald, 119, 139
recognition, employee, 83–86, 105
Republican Party, 109, 118, 129
Reserve Officer Training Corps
     (ROTC), 51
Right Stuff, The (Wolfe), 67–68
risk taking, 24–25, 28, 54, 100
Roosevelt, Theodore, 34, 118, 138
rugged individualism, 117–19,
     138–39
Rule of Three, 47–48

S

Schwarzkopf, Norman, 54, 142
statesmanship, 112
status quo, maintaining the, 20,
     24–25, 40, 54, 74
succession planning, 69–70

T

talent, innate, 2–4, 11, 28, 36, 41–
     42, 57–58, 78–79, 88, 135–37
teams
     employee recognition and, 84
     synergy, 63

training, leadership, 1–3, 27, 43–44
transfers, employee, 92
Truman, Harry, 35
trying vs. doing, 51–52
Twain, Mark, 44, 133, 141, 143

U
United States. See America
US Army, 47
US Marine Corps, 47–48

W
Washington, George, 75, 131,
    142–43
what-if exercise, 81–82
win-win solutions, 15–16
Wolfe, Tom, 67
work-from-home programs, 63–64
workloads, 48
work processes, reengineering, 95–96

Open Book Editions
A Berrett-Koehler Partner

Open Book Editions is a joint venture between Berrett-Koehler Publishers and Author Solutions, the market leader in self-publishing. There are many more aspiring authors who share Berrett-Koehler's mission than we can sustainably publish. To serve these authors, Open Book Editions offers a comprehensive self-publishing opportunity.

A Shared Mission

Open Book Editions welcomes authors who share the Berrett-Koehler mission—Creating a World That Works for All. We believe that to truly create a better world, action is needed at all levels—individual, organizational, and societal. At the individual level, our publications help people align their lives with their values and with their aspirations for a better world. At the organizational level, we promote progressive leadership and management practices, socially responsible approaches to business, and humane and effective organizations. At the societal level, we publish content that advances social and economic justice, shared prosperity, sustainability, and new solutions to national and global issues.

Open Book Editions represents a new way to further the BK mission and expand our community. We look forward to helping more authors challenge conventional thinking, introduce new ideas, and foster positive change.

For more information, see the Open Book Editions website: http://www.iuniverse.com/Packages/OpenBookEditions.aspx.

Join the BK Community! See exclusive author videos, join discussion groups, find out about upcoming events, read author blogs, and much more! http://bkcommunity.com/.

Printed in the United States
By Bookmasters